Fun With Tea

*Activities for tea loving adults
to share with their favorite young sippers.*

Compiled by Babette Donaldson

Author of The Emma Lea Books

&

Everything Healthy Tea

Published by Blue Gate Books

Fun With Tea

© 2014 Blue Gate Books, LLC

© Copyright for original art and music are held by the individual artists

ALL RIGHTS RESERVED

Publisher, Blue Gate Books and the contributing artists grant permission for the owner of this book, *Fun With Tea*, to reproduce coloring pages and song sheets for use during their own tea events as long as credit to this publication and to the artists is properly given.

This book may not be reproduced as a whole without written permission from the publisher, Blue Gate Books, the copyright holder. Permission to reproduce for commercial use may be requested from:

Permissions Editor
Blue Gate Books
P.O. Box 2137
Nevada City, CA 95959

Requests for permissions may also be submitted through the Contact link at www.Fun-With-Tea.com.

Blue Gate Books SAN: 852-923X
Library of Congress Control Number: 2014907015
ISBN13: 978-0-9792612-8-2
ISBN: 0-9792612-8-7

Blue Gate Books
www.BlueGateBooks.com

TABLE of CONTENTS

Welcome To *Fun With Tea* . . . 4

Section 1: **Tea Just For Me**

6 . . . Tea Song: "An Afternoon Tea Song"
9 . . . Coloring Page: Me, Myself & I Have Tea
11 . . . Tea Song: "When The Kettle Whistles"
12 . . . Write Your Own Tea Story
15 . . . Tea Poem: Small and Early
16 . . . Teatime Acrostic Poetry
17 . . . Tea Party Word Search
18 . . . Teatime Crossword
20 . . . Sew Your Twin Doll
22 . . . Build A Tiny Tearoom

Section 2: **Tea For Two**

24 . . . Coloring Page - "Tea for Two"
27 . . . Long Distance Tea Party For Two
28 . . . Tea Play Dough
29 . . . Painting with Tea
30 . . . Create Your Tea Blend
34 . . . Super-Easy Teapot Cozy
37 . . . Sew A Teacup
41 . . . Teapot Sweater
43 . . . Teatime Reading With Children
45 . . . Create Your Own Family Tea Times

Section 3: **Tea Party Fun**

48 . . . Tea Party Planner
50 . . . Tea Party Garland With Patterns
57 . . . Teacup Place Cards
59 . . . Small Teapot Favor Box
61 . . . Paper Teacup and Saucer Decoration
65 . . . Teapot Chinese Lamp With Patterns
71 . . . *Papier Mâché* Teapot and Teacup
77 . . . Musical Teacup Games: Six Versions
79 . . . Tea Party Mad Libs - Two Versions
82 . . . Teapot People Coloring Pages

Section 4: **Fun Teatime Recipes**

92 . . . Strawberry Flowers & Matcha Cookies
94 . . . Cambric Tea Ice Cream In A Bag
95 . . . Apple Pie Tea
96 . . . Snowflake Cinnamon Toast
97 . . . Fairy Flower Bread & Crystallized Violets
98 . . . Bas-Relief Teapot Cake
100 . . . 3-D Teapot Cake
102 . . . Homemade Fondant
103 . . . Lemon Curd & Devonshire Cream
104 . . . Mandarin Orange Scones

Section 5: **Additional Resources**

Welcome To
Fun With Tea

The intention for this activity book was to create a collection of ideas that adults can share with children to make teatime more fun. The projects and suggestions are not organized by ages or capabilities and it is not segmented for adults or children. Rather, it is assumed that adults will be sharing it with their young sippers making teatime more memorable.

How we organized the projects:

The projects are organized into three basic groups -- "Tea For Me" for solo teatimes because even children sometimes like to play alone and exercise their imaginations, "Tea For Two" includes selections for shared teatime and finally, "Tea Party Fun" for groups. There's a little something of interest for almost everyone here.

On the Website, www.Fun-With-Tea.com:

The design of the book was kept simple, black and white and was limited to the basic pattern designs - knowing that it could be expanded and interactive on the website. The site will be growing with new ideas, games and patterns almost every time you visit. *You'll find:*

- Additional tea craft projects
- Tips and tutorials
- Contests
- Ways to share your tea party art
- Galleries of your tea art photos
- Suggestions for decorating

Using the Website, www.Fun-With-Tea.com

- Go to the home page.
- Click on *"Enter Here"* under Member Login.
- Use the password - ***TSipFun4You*** - to open access to the member area.
- Subscribe to the newsletter for updates in our growing FWT community.

Can you make copies of the patterns? — Yes!

The patterns included in this print version of Fun With Tea are intended for you to trace or reproduce on a copy machine. But we've also made them available as downloadable PDFs on our website - www.Fun-With-Tea.com. You can print the patterns directly onto light cardstock or decorative paper to eliminate tracing and to keep your book intact.

Section 1

When You're Having Tea Alone

I Had A Little Tea Party
by Jessica Nelson North

*I had a little tea party this afternoon at three.
'Twas very small - Three guests in all. Just I, myself and me.*

*Myself ate all the sandwiches, while I drank up the tea;
'Twas also I who ate the pie and passed the cake to me.*

Jessica Nelson North's poem from the 1920's inspired this first section about enjoying teatime when you're alone. To expand on the idea, we commissioned songwriter, Zack David Thieman, to add the tune and additional verses, transforming North's original poem into the fun sing-along, *"An Afternoon Tea Song" (page 6)*. You'll find it on the next page along with the simple sheet music.

Activities In This Section:

Tea Song: An Afternoon Tea Song	6
Coloring Page: Me, Myself & I Have Tea	9
Tea Song: When The Kettle Whistles	11
Write Your Own Tea Story	12
Tea Poem: Small and Early by Tudor Jenks	15
Teatime Acrostic Poetry	16
Tea Party Word Search	17
Tea Party Crossword Puzzle	18
Sew Your Doll Twin	20
Build A Tiny Tearoom	22

An Afternoon Tea Song

VERSE 1: *(by Jessica North)*
I had a little tea party this afternoon at three.
It was very small, you know - Just I, myself and me.
Myself ate all the sandwiches, while I drank up the tea
It was also I who at the pie and passed the cake to me.

CHORUS:
(The remainder of the song is by Zack David Thieman)
I, myself and me make a great team
When you come to visit you will see
We're the three best friends and I'm so glad
I never have to worry 'bout feeling sad

VERSE 2:
I had a little tea party this afternoon at four
Not but a minute later and the rain began to pour
I felt so happy in my room, so cozy and so warm
While daddy's working on the shed and Mama's at the store

REPEAT CHORUS:

VERSE 3:
I had a little tea party this afternoon at five
I sat me down oh once again, just me myself and I
I ate up all the cookies and Myself let out a sigh
As me and I had failed to leave myself a piece of pie

Listen to Zack David's recording of *An Afternoon Tea Song* on our FWT website. Learn the catchy tune and sing along.

Coloring Page:
Me, Myself & I Have Tea

Coloring page created by Catherine Archer-Wills

"*Guard well your spare moments. They are like uncut diamonds. Discard them and their value will never be known. Improve them and they will become the brightest gems in a useful life.*"

By Ralph Waldo Emerson

www.Fun-With-Tea.com

When the Kettle Whistles

To the tune of "White Coral Bells"

a Traditional English Round

Lyrics by Babette Donaldson

Listen to recordings of the song on the website.

www.Fun-With-Tea.com

Write Your Own Tea Story

Coloring Page created by Catherine Archer-Wills

A Writing Prompt for Young Storytellers

Imagine that the teapot on the next page is very special and can serve anything you want. It could be something funny, or beautiful or magical. Now, write your story about the wonderful teatime that you created.

Title: _____

By: _____

_____
_____
_____
_____
_____
_____
_____
_____
_____
_____
_____
_____
_____
_____
_____
_____
_____

Would you like to illustrate your story on the next page?

www.Fun-With-Tea.com

Website password: TSipFun4You

A Tea Poem

Tudor Storrs Jenks (1857-1922) was an American journalist, artist, poet and author of many books. One of the dozens of poems published in his lifetime is this one that seems to perfectly describe an evening "playroom" teatime between father and daughter.

Originally published in An American Anthology, 1787-1900
Houghton Mifflin, Boston

Small and Early
by Tudor Jenks

When Dorothy and I took tea, we sat upon the floor;
No matter how much tea I drank, she always gave me more;
Our table was the scarlet box in which her tea-set came;
Our guests, an armless one-eyed doll, a wooden horse gone lame.
She poured out nothing, very fast, -- the teapot tipped on high,
And in the bowl found sugar lumps unseen by my dull eye.
She added rich (pretended) cream -- it seemed a willful waste,
For though she overflowed the cup, it did not change the taste.
She asked, "Take milk?" or "Sugar?" and though I answered, "No,"
She put them in, and told me that I "must take it so!"
She'd say "Another cup, Papa?" and I, "No, thank you, Ma'am,"
But then I had to take it -- her courtesy was sham.
Still, being neither green, nor black, nor English-breakfast tea,
It did not give her guests the "nerves" -- whatever those may be.
Though often I upset my cup, she only minded when
I would mistake the empty cups for those she'd filled again.
She tasted my cup gingerly, for fear I'd burn my tongue;
Indeed, she really hurt my pride -- she made me feel so young.
I must have drunk some two score cups, and Dorothy sixteen,
Allowing only needful time to pour them, in between.
We stirred with massive pewter spoons, and sipped in courtly ease,
With all the ceremony of the stately Japanese.
At length she put the cups away. "Goodnight, Papa," she said;
And I went to a real tea, and Dorothy to bed.

Teatime Acrostic Poetry

An acrostic is a poem in which the letters in a word become the first letters of a line, spelling out a word or phrase. The word or phrase you choose can be the name of a friend, a favorite flower or place, or whatever you like. Young children like to create acrostics with their own first name or the name of a family member. Here's one example with our tea activity theme:

Teatimes
by Nani Matana

Tasting
Enjoying
Allowing
Teatime
Intimacy
Mellowness
Enveloping
Senses

Now try these:

FRIEND

F _____

R _____

I _____

E _____

N _____

D _____

TEA

T _____

E _____

A _____

FAMILY

F _____

A _____

M _____

I _____

L _____

Y _____

Tea Party Word Search

Use the same words and clues from the Tea Party Crossword Puzzle.

```
U O K V H S H D V T A B L E C L O T H W M E G I P
M C O Y T I B R O W N L E M O N C U R D N N M F T
P G Z S R T B M N Z D O A L I C E O V N I S L L H
H A U R K C E I M A D H A T T E R B P B D N E U A
B R R L K A U A S S P O O N F J E E O N O S A M N
C A I T F M H J P C R E A M M D E R E M N Z V P K
R M N N Y B B V B O U P F B R T R I A O S S E H Y
I O V G F R F X Y J T S D F S E R N I C V A S F O
S W I N N I E T H E P O O H H F N T E O T G H V U
A G T R B C H M O T H E R P T I A S T V E T R A Y
V A A J T O S D S C B D O S C R A N E U A P O U R
O I T A G E E R I Y D T I X O E C H A M O M I L E
R W I M E I E W Z T S T G C L G S W T W A T E R H
I A O T K W D O S I I C E P U Y C M I B O I L Y O
E N N O O N C A R U T D H D T B O A M N A P K I N
S I O L A V O H R T I A R A N S N Y E G R E E N E
M C F S F T C F G J S A U C E R E H T E A C U P Y
```

flowers	tray	decorations	teapot	spoon
brown	green	fruit	cream	savories
toast	cambric	leaves	lemon curd	jam
chamomile	tablecloth	invitation	hibiscus	cinnamon
Christopher Robin	Mad Hatter	Winnie The Pooh	napkin	steep
saucer	tiara	cozy	lump	mint
crusts	sandwich	thank you	mother	Alice
honey	party	friends	water	boil
teatime	cookie	gaiwan	pour	tea
please	scone	milk	teacup	

Teatime Crossword

If you need a little help, check the list of clues used for the Tea Party Word Search. Each of them has been included in this Tea Party Crossword Puzzle.

Teatime Crossword, continued

Across

3. Golden syrup to sweeten tea.
4. These are sometimes removed from sandwich bread to make it look fancy.
7. Name of a British-style tea recipe that is half milk.
13. What we sometimes call the person who pours the tea even if it's not a woman.
14. How some people ask a guest if they want sugar. One _____ or two?
16. Three-piece Chinese teacup is a gai_____.
18. Make the room look like a party with _____.
21. Cloth that covers the table.
23. The part of the plant used to make tea.
24. What must be done to the water to make tea
26. Devonshire _____, often served with scones.
28. What you sip from when you drink tea.
31. What you send to ask someone to your house for tea.
33. The thing that holds the teacup.
34. Drink with jam and bread.
35. When tea is not brown, sometimes it is _____.
36. Stir your tea with a _____.
37. Something you might wave if you are wearing a fairy costume at a tea party.
38. Dairy product sometimes added to tea.
41. Almost like a crown, worn for dress-up tea parties.
42. A brown spice that is harvested from the bark of a tree and is a popular flavoring added to tea.
43. What the tea is does when you add the water and wait for about three minutes.
46. A fresh, healthy snack to serve with tea.
47. A cover to keep the teapot warm.

Down

1. Some of the people you invite to tea who are not family members.
2. What you might pick in the garden to decorate the tea table.
5. What you say when you receive something.
6. When several people are invited for teatime it quickly becomes a _____.
8. Tiny white flowers with yellow centers that brew a relaxing herbal tea.
9. Pooh Bear's human friend who comes for tea.
10. Dish that holds your sandwiches, cookies and tarts.
11. A Monster's favorite sweet treat.
12. Sweet biscuit traditionally served with afternoon cream tea.
13. Hosted a famous tea party for Alice and friends.
15. A popular green herb that flavors tea.
17. The color of most tea.
19. Young girl who drank tea with a hare and a mouse.
20. A kind of recipe served at tea parties that is not very sweet.
22. What to say when you ask for something.
25. Sweet spread made from fruit.
27. Things we use to show respect.
28. A regular time of day to have tea and snacks.
29. A popular topping for scones. Lemon _____.
30. Teddy bear who prefers to drink his tea with honey.
32. What you unfold to cover your lap.
39. A red flower often used in tea blends.
40. Bread with filling frequently served at teatime.
41. Cooked bread ready for jam.
44. What you use to serve the tea.
45. What you do when you tip the teapot to put the tea in the cup.

Sew Your Twin Doll

This is not recommended for a beginning sewer to try alone. It requires some sewing skill and is easier to make with a sewing machine.

In the 60's there was a popular pattern published by one of the sewing pattern companies to make a 3-dimensional doll about the size of a 5-year-old child. There were many children who received this beloved handmade gift and dressed it up in their hand-me-downs or shared look alike dresses. These wonderful, full-sized dolls inspired wonderful imaginary playtime and fostered the delight of being alone with your own imagination.

This version is a similar idea but we've simplified the process and made it possible for almost anyone with some sewing experience to make. Based on the familiar Kindergarten project where children help each other draw an outline of their bodies on paper, we've made it a more lasting project by using fabric rather than paper.

What you need:

- A sheet of paper large enough to trace the child's body
- Enough fabric (2-3 yards) to make a front and back of the traced body
- Permanent markers or fabric paints
- Sewing machine, thread and needles
- Polyester pillow stuffing (2-3 bags depending on the size of the doll)

Draw your doll outline:

Have the child lie down on the paper with arms and legs stretched out to the sides to trace his/her twin. Trace a rough outline, making it slightly larger than the actual body. Have the child turn both feet to the sides to draw them in silhouette.

When you have the basic outline, cut the arms and legs off of the torso.

Double the fabric and trace the pattern pieces onto the top layer. Where the arms and legs will be sewn into the body torso, add an extra 1" seam allowance that will be inserted inside the opening of the torso and top-stitched into place.

Draw in the features with permanent marker and color in the details with markers or fabric paint.

Cutting:

Cut the pieces of doubled fabric so that you have a front and back for each one.

Sewing:

With right sides together, sew the pieces together. For the torso, sew the sides and around the head but not the bottom, and leave openings to insert the arms. For the legs and arms, leave the tops open so they can be be stuffed and then inserted into the torso. Turn the torso, arms and legs so that the pieces are right-side out.

Stuffing:

Begin with the arms and legs. Fill them tightly with polyester stuffing and pin closed leaving a 1" seam allowance for inserting into the torso. Then stitch the arms and legs closed so that they remain tightly packed. Insert the arms into place inside the torso, topstitch through the four layers of fabric, completely closing the armholes. It is recommended that you stitch over this seam at least twice for reinforcement. Stitch the legs to the inside of backside of the torso, holding them in place but leaving the torso open for stuffing.

Next, stuff the torso, first filling the head and working down to the legs. When the body is tightly filled, pin the top down with the seam allowance folded inside and topstitch to close and finish the doll. It's easier to do this in two steps: sew from both sides to the middle, leaving a 2-3" space to add the last bit of stuffing. When the stuffing is tightly packed, stitch the final closure by hand.

Dressing:

The dolls easily wear regular clothes but ready-made shoes don't stay on the soft feet very well. One suggestion is to draw shoes on permanently with markers, to use a darker, sturdier fabric for shoes or to make some simple sock-like shoes out of felt that can slip on.

Option: Pattern for the more complex doll is available at: www.Fun-With-Tea.com.

Build A Tiny Tearoom

As teatime becomes a more important part of your young child's playtime, this idea might be a wonderful project to make together. Things like this tend to be some of the most remembered toys and shared moments when children look back on childhood to recall simple joys.

It's an old joke --- that the child loved the box more than the toy! In this case, recycling large appliances boxes can inspire the most creative playtimes. Children love to have their own secret spaces and it's easy to make a small inside tearoom out of a large cardboard box like a refrigerator or washing machine box. Decorate as a comfy cottage, ancient castle or Samuari warrior's meditation room. (Remember that boys enjoy teatimes and quiet spaces too.)

What you need:

- An empty, cardboard refrigerator box
- Utility knife (for adults only)
- Latex wall paint — for the surface
- Acrylic paint — to paint on details
- Paint brushes

Preparing your box:

Paint the surface of the box - inside and out if you wish. You may need two coats of paint to cover the printing on the box. Then draw where you want to put the windows and door.

Cut out the windows and door. (This is the adult job.)

Decorating:

Paint on the details to give your "tiny teahouse" its personal flair. If you're stuck for ideas, visit the website - www.Fun-With-Tea.com - for ideas and how-to suggestions.

Section 2

Tea For Two

With whom would you most like to share a cup of tea and a conversation? We've created activities in this section suggesting crafts and activities that can be shared between an adult and child considering a regular teatime an excellent opportunity to teach traditional craft skills.

Tea Limerick
by Nani Matana

My friend came over for tea
We sipped, and we laughed heartily.
We had a good time,
And made up this rhyme
"Let's do this more often," said we.

Activities In This Section:

Coloring Page: "Tea For Two"	25
Long Distance Tea Party	27
Tea Play Dough	28
Painting & Dying With Tea	29
Create Your Own Tea Blend	30
Super-Easy Tea Cozy Pattern	34
Sew A Teacup	37
Teapot Sweater	41
Teatime Reading With Children	43
Create Your Own Family Tea Times	45

Coloring Page: "Tea For Two"

Created by Catherine Archer-Wills

Complete the Picture

On the next coloring page, pretend that someone has invited you to tea.
Add yourself to the table and decorate for your private tea party

- or -

Draw an imaginary creature in the empty chair,
. . . even if it is something very silly.

Website password: TSipFun4You

www.Fun-With-Tea.com

Long Distance Tea Party

There are times when we can use tea gatherings as an incentive to disconnect from technology and the tendency to be constantly connected with phones and Internet. But, when the people who are important to us live far away, it's nice to use the same technology to connect and "be live" with video calls. This is like magic - especially to those of us who didn't grow up with easy access to friends and family who are far away. There are now several ways to schedule video calls for free or for very little. Skype and Google Hangouts are two of the best known and there are readily available tutorials for both programs. Here are some basic suggestions for sharing teatime virtually.

Practice making a video call:

Watch the tutorials, take notes and then practice making a call before scheduling your tea party.

Create your plan:

Start with the basics: day and time, theme and menu. You may want a simple tea-for-two or a much larger group. With a large group, one person should be designated as the moderator for the call.

Send the invitations:

If you are sending snail mail invitations, consider including a teabag so that your guest share the same flavor. You might share recipes for the treats. The idea is to have everyone enjoying the same tea and treats.

More elaborate:

Prepare treats that are easy to mail and create a tea party in a box along with the teacups. Suggest that your guest has the water simmering before the call but opens their box at the same time, brews their tea and enjoys the treats.

Set a time to begin and to end:

Like any party, it's good to have a basic idea of what you plan to do and how long it will take.

What's different about a video call and a video tea party?

Just as an afternoon snack can be made more special and memorable by calling it teatime, sharing tea with friends, as you meet via video calls is transformed by the intention of teatime and the extra effort you add to make it special.

Record the call:

Some of the video calling services provide the tools to record your session. Like a home movie, this is one way to save memories of our older family members to pass along to the next generations.

Tea Play Dough

Manipulating play dough is already a sensory experience but adding the color and aroma of tea to our make-it-yourself recipe increases the pleasure for children as well as adults. Most of these ingredients are items in the cupboard so this can be a quick-fix rainy-day activity.

Ingredients:

2   cups sifted flour

1   cup cornstarch

1   cup salt

2   tablespoons cream of tartar

2   cups strongly brewed tea

2   tablespoons vegetable oil

    Food coloring, if desired

Directions:

In a large saucepan, whisk together the dry ingredients, then add the liquids. Continue to whisk until the slurry is smooth. Then put the pan over low heat and stir until it begins to gather into a ball. This takes 5-10 minutes. (Some have adapted this for a slow cooker but the cooking time is considerably longer.)

Turn the dough out onto a counter or breadboard and knead it as you would knead bread dough until it is very smooth. This is a good time to add color and scented oils so you may want to knead with plastic gloves. Store in a covered or sealed container for about 2 weeks.

Knead it again when you're ready to use it.

Some suggestions for tea flavors:

- Mint herbal tea
- Orange spice black tea
- Chai black tea with Spices
- Rooibos herbal tea
- Hibiscus herbal tea (also adds color)
- Berry blends with tea
- Green tea with matcha powder
- Lemon tea with lemon juice

Projects & playtime suggestions:

By adding color and aroma, children enjoy using this tea scented and colored play dough to make food items. This makes it an especially good "pretend" teatime craft. Varying the color quickly suggests certain vegetables and fruits. Spice scents are easy to imagine as cookies and cakes.

Painting & Dying With Tea

There is an old tradition of dying white fabric with black tea to give it a soft ivory color. Many of the botanicals we use to brew herbal tea are also used as dye. Here we are also suggesting that some can be used like watercolor paint to make lovely, sepia toned paintings.

Preparing the tea paint:

Boil your teas and herbs to make strong concentrations. The amount of tea and the length of time will vary, depending on the darkness of the color with which you wish to paint. Black tea will give you sepia tones. Hibiscus flowers will be a brilliant red. Dried blueberries can become a soft purple. Green tea doesn't always stay green when it's boiled. Sometimes it turns reddish.

Painting on paper:

The best paper is a very porous watercolor paper. A glossy surface will not absorb the tea paint well. When painting, you can add water to small portions to thin and dilute your paint to help create shading. Look at a copy of an old-fashioned sepia photograph as an example.

Suggestion: Use your tea-painted watercolor paper to make some of the paper crafts in Fun With Tea.

Dying with Tea:

Boil your tea and herbs to make a strong solution. (Example: 5-6 black tea bags per gallon of water) Let it steep until cold. Add 2 tablespoons of vinegar and 2 tablespoons of salt, stirring until completely dissolved.

Remove the teabags or strain the tea since loose leaves can make a darker spot on your cloth. Test a swatch of fabric in your dye before using it on your main fabric - tea only works on natural fibers. Most synthetic fibers do not accept the color.

Moisten your fabric completely. Then, submerge the fabric so that it covers all the surfaces evenly - adding a weight if necessary - and let it sit in the tea dye bath for at least an hour, or longer for a darker color. A faster method is to boil the fabric in the pot with the tea. This works for small pieces but may not be practical for larger ones.

Rinse with cold water and a light soap solution. Tea dyed fabric will fade a bit with each wash.

Create Your Own Tea Blends

An array of colors, textures and aromas can make children feel like they're concocting a magic potion as they blend a bit and a pinch of fun. Creating your own family flavors by experimenting with your favorite flavors might become holiday gifts, packaged in decorative containers.

These are a few of the tea herbs and spices frequently found in herbal tea blends:

- Acai
- Allspice
- Apple - dried bits
- Barley - roasted
- Bee Balm
- Blueberries - dried
- Carob
- Chamomile
- Chrysanthemum
- Cinnamon bark
- Cloves
- Cocoa powder
- Coconut
- Cranberries - dried
- Echinacea root
- Elderberry
- Ginger
- Ginger root
- Hibiscus
- Honeybush
- Horehound
- Jasmine flowers
- Lavender
- Licorice root
- Lemon Balm
- Lemon peel
- Lemon Verbena
- Lime peel
- Orange peel
- Peppermint
- Raspberry leaves
- Rooibos
- Rose hips
- Rosemary
- Rose petals or buds
- Spearmint
- Stevia
- Tea - green, black, white, oolong, etc.
- Tulsi
- Tumeric
- Vanilla bean
- Wintergreen leaf
- Woodruff

Including children in food preparation almost always offers an opportunity to talk about nutrition and selecting good quality food. Activities such as blending teas also open us to greater sensory experiences and realizing more ways to enjoy our food. By blending your own herbs and spices, you're creating a quality beverage to your own taste, knowing exactly what's been added — or not.

How to begin:

Start with familiar favorites. Almost everyone knows the taste of cinnamon and orange as a flavored tea, or lemon and mint, apples and berries. Choose a dominant flavor and make this the foundation of your blend. As you consider other flavors, try to imagine what they might taste like together.

For your first blends, limit your ingredients, perhaps just 3 - 4, so that you can distinctly taste each of the flavors in your blend. It helps to brew a sampling of a new or long-forgotten flavor before you try it in a blend. For example, Tulsi (also known as Holy Basil) is very popular in tea blends. You may have tasted it in combination with other flavors. But you will probably be happier with your final result if you prepare and taste it separately first, before blending it with anything else.

Going shopping:

Most health food stores now stock wide varieties of herbs for blending your own teas. Go with a prepared list of ingredients you know you want but then take time to explore other possibilities. Tea blending and brewing is a sensory experience and the more we remain open to all possibilities, the more exciting it becomes and the more we benefit from tea drinking.

Can you play a guessing game in the store? Fill the bag with a well-known flavor and then ask your companions - children and adults - to guess the name by smell alone.

Weights and measures:

If you were to weigh the crushed contents in teabags designed to brew an 8-ounce mug, you would find that the net weight of the botanical materials is between 2 and 4 grams. We sometimes think of measuring tea for a single cup as a heaping teaspoon. But when we begin to blend herbs, it's very difficult to do so in these small quantities. So, we usually create blends in slightly larger quantities - so that you end up with about 1 cup of your dry blend.

Depending on the accuracy you want, you may be very happy with measuring by teaspoons and tablespoons or you may want to use a digital gram scale to measure by weight rather than by volume.

Continued, page 32

Create Your Own Tea Blends, continued

Fractions:

You can translate your recipe for your tea blend into different quantities if you think of your ingredients as percentages of the whole amount you want to create. An example would be this lemon-chamomile tea: 50% lemon grass, 20% chamomile, 10% lemon peel, 10% lemon balm. In this blend, the tartness of the three lemon ingredients is sweetened by a generous amount of chamomile. Using the percentage method allows you to mix a batch small enough for personal use or large enough to brew gallons.

Crushing herbs:

Using a mortar and pestle, you can crush hard spices or large flowers into finer grains that infuse more quickly and more easily fill teabags. This is an old-fashioned piece of equipment that is fun for kids and adults. There are also various kinds of grinders that can help you prepare your blend, if needed.

Flavoring:

One method used to flavor teas is to add a liquid essence - oil or concentrate. The easiest way to use this is to allow a few drops to coat the inside of a clean jar. Add your dry blend, shake it vigorously and then allow it to sit for 12 - 24 hours. Shake occasionally during this time. Note that using good quality flavoring is as important as using healthy botanicals. Poor quality flavoring components can have an unpleasant aftertaste.

Scenting:

If you've ever tasted Jasmine Tea, you've tasted a scented tea. To make it, the dry tea is stored with freshly picked flowers until the tea absorbs the scent. Then they are separated. This is also done with other kinds of flowers that are not as well known. You can use this same technique with some of your aromatic edible flowers such as roses and and chrysanthemum. It's also possible to scent your tea with a whole cinnamon stick or vanilla bean.

Storage:

Your tea will retain its flavor and healthful qualities if it is stored in an airtight container, in a cool place where it will not be degraded by direct sunlight. Herbs should all be stored in airtight containers until you're ready to use them.

Filling your own teabags:

There are several styles and sizes of fill-yourself-teabags. The one thing to remember is to pack the tea loosely. Most have a flap that can be folded over or they are tall enough to tie in a knot. The filter material is usually thin and porous enough to pierce with a short wooden skewer that spans the top of your cup and suspends the tea in the water. This top section can also be tied closed with a bit of colored embroidery floss and is usually long enough to drape over the side of the cup.

Tips For A Tea-Blending Party

What you enjoy sharing with your own family can easily become a party. Everyone can make their own recipe for a blended tea, compare flavors and go home with a batch of their creation. What a healthy party activity!

- If you're organizing a group to blend teas, it is easier to measure by teaspoons rather than by weight. Make tags for each ingredient and provide a separate spoon in each bowl.

- Have your guests select 3-4 of their favorite ingredients, measuring a full, half or "pinch" of each into their own cups.

- Suggest that they write the recipes on a card so that, if they like it, they can make more. Or, if it's not quite right, they can make adjustments.

- Mix the ingredients thoroughly, shaking the cup or stirring with spoons.

- Give each guest a fill-it-yourself teabag.

- Measure a heaping spoonful to the bag and tie it closed with a piece of thin, white thread or colored embroidery floss.

- Brew a cup of tea with each blend.

- Pour a small amount of each one into individual tasting cups (or disposable condiment cups).

- Consider making it a blind tasting with the samples numbered.

- Can the guests guess their own blend? Which ones are the favorites?

- Finally, mix another batch of the best recipes and serve with the party snacks.

- Have enough dry ingredients and fill-it-yourself teabags that guests can make extras to take home.

Super-Easy Teapot Cozy

We wanted to design a very simple beginner's sewing project that doesn't require a sewing machine or with much experience. This is it! All you need is a needle and thread that matches your soft, cushy fabric. *In fact, this is so quick and easy, it could be a home tea party activity or a children's class in a tearoom.*

What you need:

- ¼ yard of heavyweight polar fleece
- Notions: thread, pins, needles, scissors

Cutting the fabric:

Fold one edge of the polar fleece over enough to cut one piece. Pin the pattern to cut out the first side. Repeat for the second side. (Note: since polar fleece doesn't unravel, there's no need to finish the raw edge.)

Sewing:

Matching the two sides, pin together. Use a simple running stitch to sew the curved arch. Thread the needle. Double the thread and knot the end. Starting at one side, push the needle through the two pieces and pull it all the way through. Then, about ¼" to the side, push the needle back through and pull tight. Continue making these same stitches all around the arch. At the end, be sure to tie a knot to secure the stitches.

Finishing:

Turn the cozy inside out so the row of stitches don't show. Now your cozy is ready for teatime.

Check the website for variations of this simple pattern: www.Fun-With-Tea.com.

Super-Easy Teapot Cozy, *continued*

Reduce or enlarge to fit your teapot.

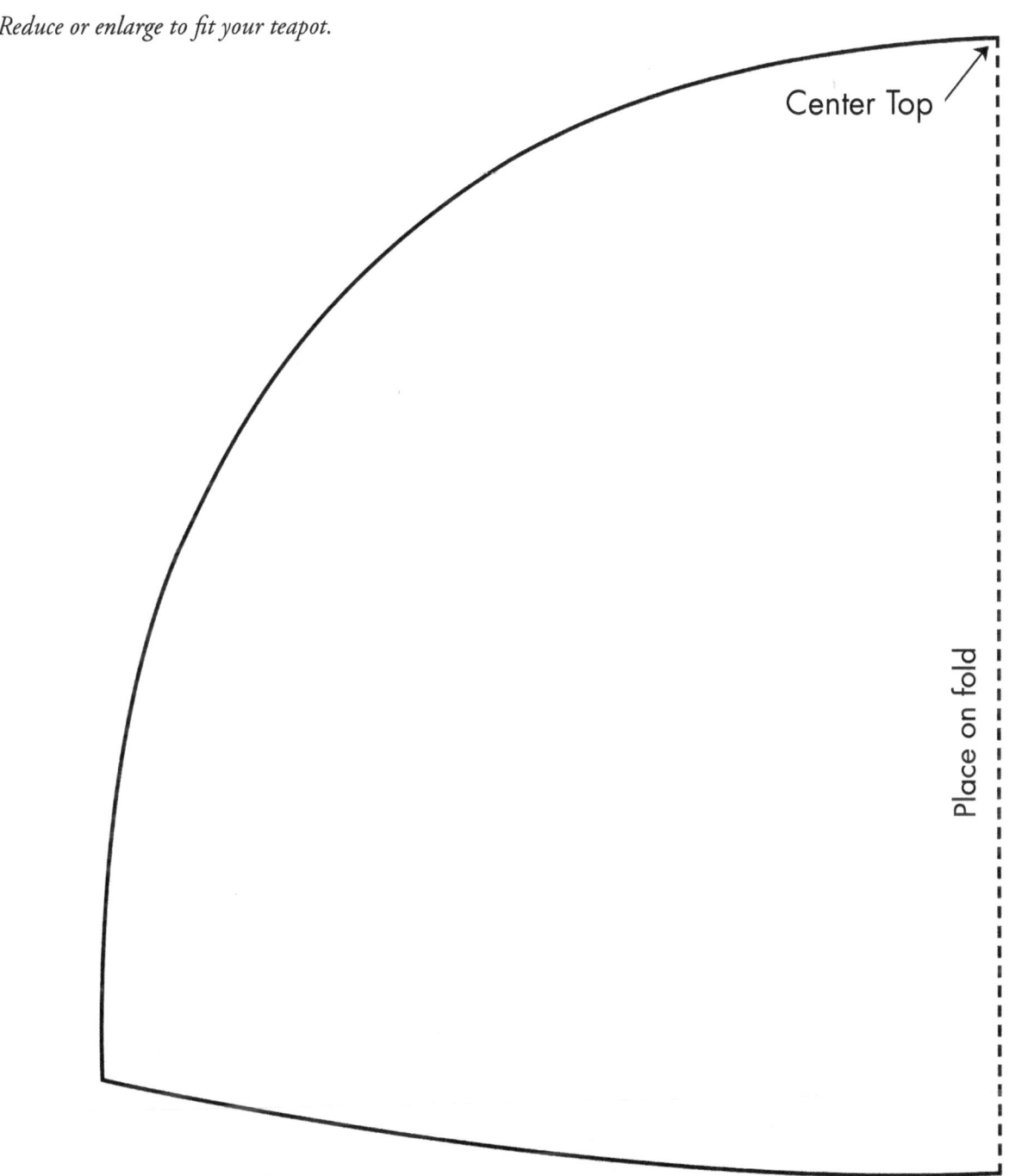

www.Fun-With-Tea.com

Sew A Teacup

This is a great project for a quilter or seamstress who has a "stash" of colorful fabrics and boxes of scrap pieces too good to throw away. It can become a wonderful toy tea set or an inexpensive party favor. It's not a beginner project but after you make one, the second one will be a snap. Having a sewing machine and some experience is helpful.

What you need:

- Fabric - approximately ½ yard total. This can be mix-and-match pieces and scraps.
- Sewing thread
- Pipe cleaner - the length of your handle
- Batting - lightweight
- Fusible inner facing (optional)
- 14-16" of double-folded bias tape

Selecting your fabric:

Almost any fabric will work just fine but some of the colorful cottons are lightweight and may need reinforcement or batting to hold the shape. A medium weight corduroy, velvet or even blue jean denim are fabrics that stand up well on their own.

Cutting the pieces:

For the teacup, cut 10 pieces of the triangle pattern for the teacup -- 5 for the inside and 5 for the outside. They can be the same fabric or different. If you're using inner facing or batting, cut those additional pieces as needed. For the saucer, cut 2 pieces of fabric and 1 of batting for the large circle. Cut 2 pieces of fabric for the small circle. Cut 1 piece for the handle.

Making your handle:

Sew the handle fabric along the longer side with right sides together. Using a large safety pin or knitting needle, turn it right-sides-out. Fit your pipe cleaner inside to help the handle hold its shape. Fold the ends inside and stitch it closed so that the rough edges of the fabric won't show. Bend it into the curved "C" shape for your handle.

Sewing your teacup:

Sew the five triangles together, keeping right sides together, for the inner cup and for the outer cup, allowing a 1/4" seam allowance. Press the seams flat and then invert the inner cup and fit it inside the outer cup with the wrong sides together - so that the two right sides are both showing.

"Stitch the ditch" of 2 or 3 of the side seams to secure inside and outside together. Then glue or topstitch the rim of the teacup to make it easier to attach the trim. Then gently push the bottom center up into the inside of the cup to flatten the base. If it doesn't hold the shape for the bottom, secure with a couple of stitches.

Sew the double-fold bias tape over the two layers of the rim. Allow the ends to overlap about 3/4" but don't stitch it down. Tuck the raw edge under and secure it with a few blind stitches. Add your finished handle with a few stitches to each end.

Sewing the saucer:

Small Circle: Match the 2 pieces of the small circle with right sides together. Stitch around the edge with a ¼" seam allowance, leaving about 1" open to turn it right sides out. Stitch the opening and then press it flat.

Large Circle: Match the batting of the large circle to the wrong side of one of the fabric pieces and baste into place. Then, align the two large circles with wrong sides together and stitch around the circle with a ¼" seam allowance, leaving a 1½" opening to turn the right sides out. Stitch the opening closed and then press flat.

Center the smaller circle in the middle of the larger circle. Pin securely and then stitch it into place. Either blind stitch the edge of the small circle or use a sewing machine with a sharp needle to stitch through the 5 layers of fabric.

Sew a Teacup, *continued*

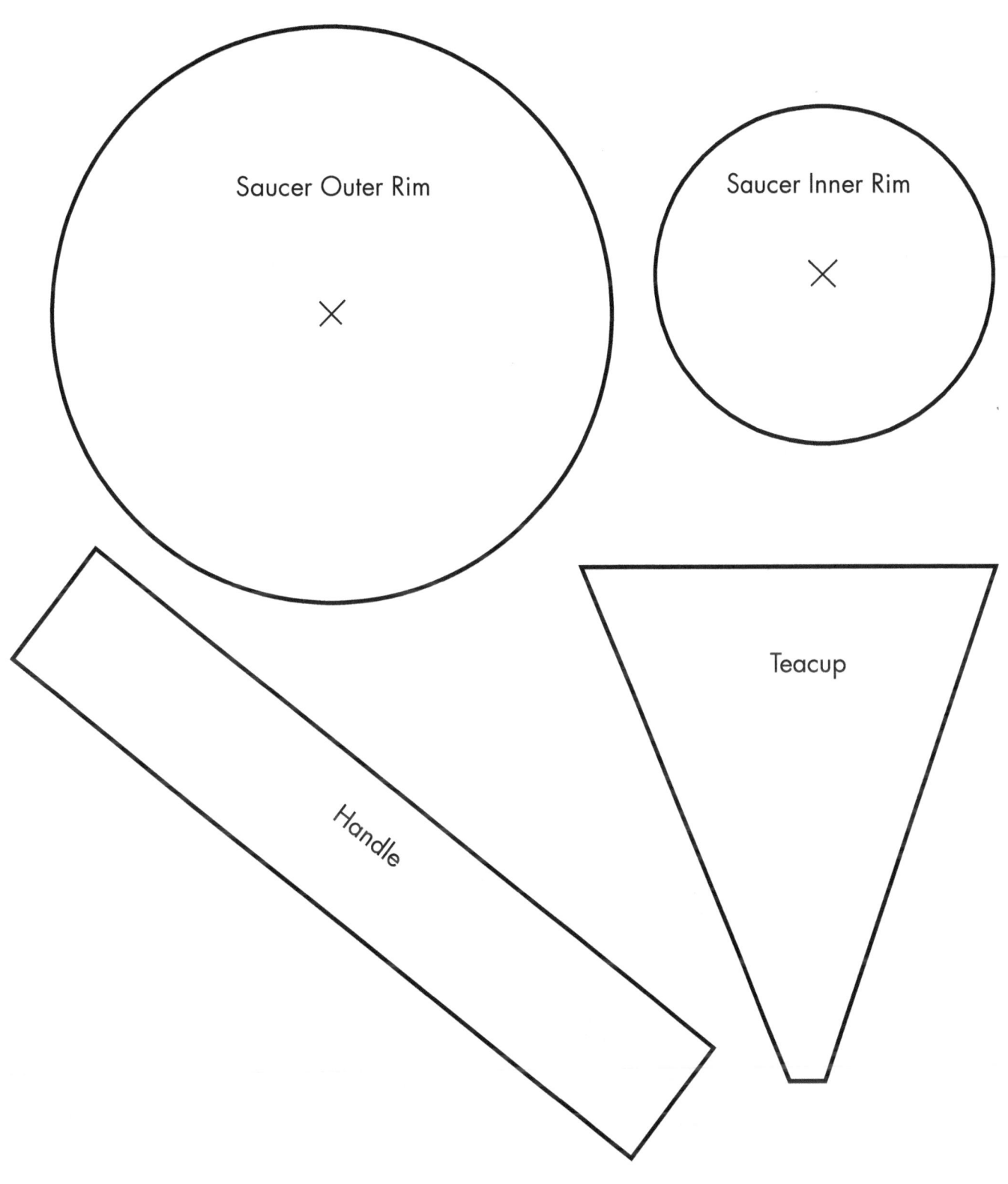

www.Fun-With-Tea.com

Teapot Sweater

The only knitting stitches needed for this pattern are knit, purl and knit-together. A first-time knitter can practice with these basics and finish the project quickly.

There's something about sitting down to work on needlecrafts with a cup of tea as a companion that traditionally go together. For that reason, it is included in the section, "Tea For Two". Afternoon teatime can also be an excellent time to teach the creative arts and this little pattern is an excellent starter project - especially for younger crafters. We've written the instructions so that it can be custom-fitted to almost any teapot and made suggestions for whimsical decorations. While the regular name for this would be a cozy, the fact that it's knitted and custom fitted, we like to call it a sweater.

What you need:

- ½ skein, 8 ply wool
- Size 6, 12" straight needles
- 1 yard decorative ribbon that matches the yarn (½" wide)
- 1 tapestry needle
- 1 large stitch holders
- Fabric glue

Finding your gauge:

Knit a test piece by casting on 24 stitches and then knitting 4-6 rows. Measure the width of the test swatch. Count how many stitches per inch. This will vary with the weight of the wool, the size of the needles and the tension of the knitter. Once you know how many stitches per inch you will knit, then measure or calculate the circumference of the base of the teapot.

Circumference = π (3.14) x Diameter

Continued, page 42

Teapot Sweater, *continued*

Begin knitting:

Cast on the number of stitches that you calculated will equal the circumference of the base of your teapot. Then knit two complete rows.

At the 3rd row, purl the entire row and begin to alternate every row in stockingette stitch until you reach the base of the spout. This will be about 1" or 4-5 rows.

When you reach what would be the base of the spout, knit or purl half of that row (continuing in stockingette). Place the remaining half of the stitches on a stitch holder.

Continue until you reach the distance that represents the top of the spout. This will be 2-3". At this point, place the stitches just finished on the other stitch holder and cut the yarn leaving an 8" piece for stitching sides together.

Place the other half of the saved stitches on the stitch holder back on the needle and continue in stockingette to match the other side.

When you've completed the number of rows that will be at the point where the top of the spout connects to the teapot, preferably stopping after completing a purl row, place all of the stitches back onto one needle and continue the pattern until the teapot begins to decrease.

With the right side facing you, knit 5, knit 2 together until end of row.

Purl the next row completely without reducing the stitches.

Next row, knit 4, knit 2 together until end of row. Then purl next row.

Next row, knit 3, knit 2 together until end of row. Then purl next row.

Next row, knit 2, knit 2 together until end of row. Then purl next row.

Next row, knit 1, knit 2 together until end of row. Then purl next row.

Final rows - knit 2 together until end of row and continue until 5-10 stitches remain. Cut the yarn leaving an 8" piece. Using a tapestry needle, pull the yarn through the remaining stitches on the needle. Slip the stitches off the needle and pull tight. Sew the handle-side seam closed down to the top of the handle.

Bottom closure:

Secure the ribbon in place with a bit of glue and allow it to dry. This will make it easier to stitch the ribbon in a straight line. When the glue is dry, sew the ribbon around the bottom, either inside or outside, leaving the ends long enough to tie in a bow.

Teatime Reading With Children

Teatime is wonderful for reading and is one of the most important and memorable activities we can share with our children. The two lists we've compiled here are examples of some of the most popular and beloved teatime stories. We've separated them into the classics and into books written with a tea theme.

Classics

- *Aesop's Fables*
- *Alice's Adventures in Wonderland* by Lewis Carroll
- *Anderson's Fairy Tales* by Hans Christian Anderson
- *Anne of Green Gables* by Lucy Maud Montgomery
- *Are You My Mother?* by P.D. Eastman
- *A Wrinkle In Time (The Time Quintet Series)* by Madeleine L'Engle
- *Bed-Knob and Broomsticks* by Mary Norton
- *Blueberries for Sal* by Robert McCloskey
- *Charlotte's Web* by E.B. White
- *In The Night Kitchen* by Maurice Sendak
- *Little Women* by Louisa May Alcott
- *Madeline* by Ludwig Bemelmans
- *Redwall* by Brian Jacques (And the entire *Redwall Series*)
- *Rikki-Tikki-Tavi* by Rudyard Kipling
- *Stuart Little* by E.B. White
- *The Adventures of Tom Sawyer* by Mark Twain
- *The Borrowers* by Mary Norton
- *The Cat In The Hat* by Dr. Seuss
- *The Complete Tale* of Peter Rabbit by Beatrix Potter
- *The Giving Tree* by Shel Silverstein
- *The Jungle Book* by Rudyard Kipling
- *The Lion, the Witch and the Wardrobe* by C.S. Lewis
- *The Wind In the Willows* by Kenneth Grahame
- *The Secret Garden* by Frances Hodgson Burnett
- *The Snowy Day* by Ezra Jack Keats

Tea-Themed Books For Children

- *Ava's Secret Tea Party* (Littlest Angels) by Donna J Shepherd and Bella Sinclair
- Dora Books: *Let's Have a Tea Party!* by Llanit Oliver and Victoria Ying
- Dora Books: *Tea Party in Wonderland* by Llanit Oliver and Victoria Ying
- Emma Lea Books: *Emma Lea's First Tea Party* by Babette Donaldson
- Emma Lea Books: *Emma Lea's Magic Teapot* by Babette Donaldson
- Emma Lea Books: *Emma Lea's Tea With Daddy* by Babette Donaldson
- Emma Lea Books: *Emma Lea's First Tea Ceremony* by Babette Donaldson
- Fancy Nancy: *Tea for Two* by Jane O'Connor
- Fancy Nancy: *Tea Parties* by Jane O'Connor
- *I'm A Little Teapot* by Iza Trapini
- *Let's Have A Tea Party!* by Emilie Barnes, Sue Christian Parsons and Michael Sparks
- *Madeline's Tea Party* by John Bemelmans Marciano
- *Miss Spider's Tea Party: The Counting Book*
- *Mr. Putter & Tabby Pour The Tea* by Cynthia Ryland and Arthur Howard
- *My Little Pony: The World's Biggest Tea Party*
- *Nature's Royal Tea Party* by Cheryl Kling
- *Olivia Plans a Tea Party* by Natalie Shaw
- *Ruby's Tea for Two* by Rosemary Wells
- *Sun Kissed Sweet Tea* by Mia Alexander-Davis and Crystal Swain
- *Tea Cakes for Tosk* by Kelly Starling Lyons and E.B. Lewis
- *Tea Ceremony* by Shozo Sato
- *Tea For Ruby* by Sarah Ferguson, Duchess of York.
- *Tea For Ten* by Lena Anderson and Elizabeth Kallick Dyssegaard
- *Tea Leaves* by Frederick Lipp and Lester Coloma
- *Tea Party Today: Poems To Sip and Savor* by Eileen Spinelli and Karen Dugan
- *Tea Party Rules* by Ame Dyckman
- *Tea With an Old Dragon* by Jane Yolen
- *Tea With Grandpa* by Barney Saltzbert
- *Tea With Hazel* by Jada Fitch
- *Tea With Imaginary Friends* by John Ornellas
- *Tea With Lady Sapphire* by Carl R Sams and Jean Stoick
- *Tea With Milk* by Allen Say
- *Tea With Rex* by Molly Idle
- *Tea Parties With Grandma* by Barbara McNair and Eric Hogan
- *Tea Party For Two* by Michelle Poploff
- *The Perfect Princess Tea Party Read-Along Storybook* by Kitty Richards (Disney)
- *The Tiger Who Came To Tea* by Judith Kerr
- *Washday* by Eve Bunting

Create Your Own Family Tea Times

What is Family Tea Time?

We create a setting for conversation and relaxation. We behave with respect and courtesy. We listen. We pay attention to the small details. In so doing, everyone who joins us at the table feels important. We can make it easy. We make it fun. In doing so, we make it memorable.

We turn off the television, abandon all electronics, don't answer phones and shift our focus to the people in our lives. Small talk is critical. Laughter sweetens the cup. For a few minutes we set aside our worries and share a bit of joy.

Make It Fun:

- Bedtime teas can be relaxing family rituals when teatime is a read-aloud story time.
- Craft activities pair well with teatime. It can be the designated hour when adults share their favorite hobbies and crafts such as drawing, painting, knitting, crochet, sewing, quilting, weaving, woodcarving, lapidary, jewelry making, paper making and more.
- Teatime can be based on special themes with costumes or silly dress-up.
- Family traditions can also include visits to local tearooms. Many have special events including special holiday tea parties.
- Teatime can be inside or outside. Consider a short hike and a simple teatime picnic. In regions with winter snow activities such as skiing, there are often snowshoeing trails with warming cabins where a backpack full of tea things can be shared.
- Children love to be included in the planning and preparations as much as they enjoy being surprised.

Make It Healthy:

- Flavored teas with fruit essences and sweet spices are aromatic and usually taste sweet enough to satisfy a craving even without sugar or additional sweeteners. These can easily replace popular sodas and sweetened juice drinks.
- Consider the health benefits of some of the herbal teas as well as true tea, Camellia sinensis. The herb shelf in your local market or health food store is a bit of an apothecary in disguise. Ancient healing lore may inspire you to plant an herb garden to grow your own tea ingredients.
- Set the scene to encourage relaxation. Eliminate distractions and focus on positive conversation, sharing stories and ideas. Make it a time that every member of the family looks forward to.
- While all true tea is high in antioxidants, some teas such as powdered Matcha, is considerably higher because of the way it is made. Matcha tea products have become more available, more affordable and easier to serve.
- Use tea's sensory components to stimulate a young child's senses. Smell the aroma, look at the color of the tea and the shapes of the whole leaves, taste the subtle flavors, listen to the sounds of the kettle boiling, wrap fingers around a warm cup and touch the whole, wet leaf that has been restored like magic.

Family Tea Times, *continued*

Make It Affordable:

- It can be very inexpensive to create a mix-and-match tea set by shopping at yard sales and thrift stores. Everyone can have their own cup and tea can be served from a real teapot.

- Many tea foods are simple, such as regular sandwiches that have been embellished. It's easy to remove the crusts or cut shapes with large cookie cutters.

- Select dried edible flowers, herbs and spices from the health food store's bulk section and mix your own flavors.

- There are probably ingredients in your cupboard that, with a little imagination, can become special teatime treats. Graham crackers, chocolate sauce, peanut butter, dried fruit snacks, fresh fruit, cinnamon and bread for toast.

Make It Easy:

- Give everyone a job. Share the preparation and cleanup. Even young children can feel grown-up when they share the responsibilities for setting the table or pouring the tea.

- When you make a batch of cookies, roll some of the dough in a log shape so that it can be frozen and sliced and baked fresh so that you can serve hot cookies in minutes.

- Use a cozy to keep your teapot warm at the table. Then relax and enjoy the conversation.

- Teabags! Don't be concerned about opting for the convenience of teabags and the fun of the hundreds of different flavor options.

Make It Memorable:

- Serve traditional recipes that have been passed down for generations and share the family stories.

- Set aside a regular time for tea and conversation. Turn off the TV and phones. Let everyone who joins you know they are important enough to have your undivided attention.

- Be careful to include everyone in the conversation. No one is more important than another. Everyone's voice needs to be heard. This includes parents. Make teatime special by sharing stories from your own childhood.

- Only plan what you can accomplish comfortably, without stress. It's the laughter and comfortable times together that make the most cherished memories.

Section 3

Tea Party Fun

There are many ways to celebrate with tea parties - from extremely simple to very formal. Perhaps the most fun is had in creating the event and sharing preparations. What we've included here are just a few ideas to help you get started. Hopefully, each suggestion will inspire your own creative adaptations. Don't hesitate to adapt our songs, games, crafts and recipes and make them your own!

A Proper Tea is much nicer than a Very Nearly Tea, which is one you forget about afterwards.

From *Winnie-the-Pooh* by A. A. Milne

Activities In This Section:

Tea Party Planner	48
Tea Party Garland With Teapot & Teacup Patterns	50
Teacup Place Cards	57
Small Teapot Favor Box	59
Paper Teacup & Saucer	61
Teapot Chinese Lamp	65
Papier Mâché Teapot and Teacup	71
Musical Teacup Games	77
Tea Party Mad Lib	79
Teapot People Coloring Pages	81

Tea Party Planner

The following suggestions are written for those hosting a fairly large tea party. We've focused on the details that, if you plan well ahead of time, will make your event run more smoothly. This is especially important when planning events for young children.

1. Do you have a theme? It's not necessary, but it can add to the fun! This list is included to inspire your own creativity. The theme can be expressed in decorations, food and activities. It may encourage dress-up and also be a bit educational.

    - Winter Holiday Elegant Tea
    - Holiday Comfy Tea - A respite for the season
    - Mother-Daughter Tea Party
    - Ladies of the Family (all ages)
    - Birthday Tea
    - Garden Party
    - Everything Flowers Tea
    - Rose Tea Party
    - Spring Fling
    - Musical Tea Party
    - Dance Tea Party
    - Ladybug Tea
    - Teddy Bear Tea
    - Circus Tea Party
    - "Little Women" - Literary Theme
    - Jane Austen - Author Theme
    - Beatrix Potter - Peter Rabbit Tea
    - Princess Party
    - Disney Princesses Reunion
    - Samuari Warrior Tea (for boys)
    - Cowboy & Cowgirl Tea Party
    - Pirate Tea
    - Halloween Witches & Goblins Tea
    - Mad Hatter & Alice Tea
    - Fancy Nancy Tea
    - Wizard of OZ Party
    - Mary Poppins Tea
    - Harry Potter Party
    - Zoo Animal Tea Party
    - Fairy Tale Dress-Up Tea
    - Valentine Tea
    - "In The Pink" Get Well Tea
    - Japanese Tea Ceremony- Simplified
    - Pajama Tea Party
    - Dora, The Explorer Tea
    - Hobbit Tea Party - "Second Breakfast"
    - Snow Tea - Celebrate the winter
    - A Just-Because Tea - for no special reason whatsoever

2. Plan your main menu items first. Consider serving and decorating foods that you can incorporate into the theme, if you use one.

3. Plan where and how you will serve the tea and food.
   - Will it be a buffet or will everything be served on the table?
   - If something on your menu plan presents a problem with serving it (such as keeping something warm or cold) consider changing that item to make your serving easier.
   - Do you have enough people to help? Arrange for an extra pair of helping hands in case of an emergency or someone else not showing up?
   - How many people can you comfortably seat and serve according to your plan?
   - Are any of your guests likely to bring a surprise guest at the last minute? Will you have room? Do you have to make your invitation clear about the size of the party?
   - If you're serving a large crowd, consider how you will serve the tea. It can be a bit tricky to serve hot tea to a crowd - especially if you are offering several choices.

4. Prepare a guest list and send invitations (mail, email or phone) about three weeks before your party day.

5. Give yourself enough time to prepare your decorations and plan how they will be hung and/or placed. Do you need help? How much can you do in advance? A list can be a great asset. Schedule the day, time and helpers you might need.

6. Have you made the recipes before? Do you need to practice? Are there items that can be made ahead and frozen? Will you have some of the guests bring their specialties? If so, is it a balanced menu with plenty of variety?

7. Prepare a seating chart for the guests, another detailed plan showing where the prepared food will be kept prior to serving, and, if you plan to serve a buffet, make a simple map of the table indicating where each dish will be placed.

8. Do an advance walk-through with your helpers.

9. Post a schedule for your tea party including who is assigned each task and the time it should happen. Make sure it is easily seen, perhaps in a couple of places. For large events, have one person tasked with keeping everyone on track.

10. Party favors? Some of your decorations can double as small, take-home gifts. It might be something as simple as the place card with the guest's name. Or, if you served your own special tea blend, package a small amount for each guest.

11. Photos of your event are important. Make sure everyone is included. If the tea party becomes an annual event, the photos are important reminders of how you organized and will help you make decisions about what to do differently.

12. If you think that you will have annual or regular tea parties, consider what equipment and decorations can be used again. If you're on a budget, this will make every year a little easier and more economical.

13. Plan to have fun. If you have organized well, the fun naturally follows. (Especially for children's parties.) Enjoy yourself so much that you're excitedly anticipating the next tea even before the current one has ended.

14. Clean Up! It's nice to have a few designated volunteers (or hire an assistant) who have not been on their feet for the whole tea party to come in at the end to tidy up.

Tea Party Garland

This festive idea can be used in many ways - as a simple and inexpensive decoration or as a craft project during a children's tea party, as part of a game or as a small take-home party favor.

What you need:

- Colorful cardstock or heavyweight paper
- Ribbon or other material for the string
- Markers or crayons
- Glue (optional)

Using the simple teapot and teacup patterns, trace or photocopy onto your paper. Cut them out and space them evenly along the ribbon or string. You can alternate the teapots and teacups or use only one pattern. Tying a loose knot in the string or securing it with a bow or a bit of glue helps keep them from sliding.

What we like about this project:

- This is an inexpensive decoration that can easily be stored and used repeatedly if you have regular tea party events or fundraisers.
- Children can participate by coloring and decorating.
- There are many creative variations on the basic instructions.

Option 1: Use colorful, decorative paper that you might find in craft supply stores for scrapbook art. Selecting the right size paper or cutting paper to fit into your printer allows you to print directly onto the paper, eliminating the tracing step.

Tea Party Garland, *continued*

Option 2: You can print the names of your guests on the teapots or teacups, perhaps adding a little thank-you on the backside as a take home party favor. If you want to use the decorations during the party, one way to remove them quickly and easily is to make two and glue them at the top so they slip over the ribbon and hang down.

Option 3: Print tea quotes by famous people on the surface to entertain your guests. There are quotes from children's literature, by those characters and authors, as well as quotes by authors who write for adults. (We've included some popular quotes in Section 5 - Resources, page 106.)

Option 4: Use the teapot garland to decorate a tree for your event so that it looks like a Christmas tree - no matter what the season! This looks better with smaller teapots and teacups so just reduce the pattern with a photocopier.

Option 5: Rather than using ribbon they can be tied in the spaces between the bulbs of cool, LED decorative lights. Use ribbon to tie them on, letting them dangle a bit so they move with a bit of breeze.

Option 6: Create your garland by decorating a teapot or teacup each time you have tea together. Beginning with the first one, you might jot a note about what you did together, what tea you served, who joined you as guests or write out your entire menu. Then, every time you have tea together, bring it out and add another piece to your garland and plan to hang it at your next tea.

Option 7: Use the cinnamon and applesauce dough rather than paper to add to your garland, giving a sweet, spicy scent to the room. These also make nice gifts. But you will probably want to reduce the size of the patterns we've provided or find cookie cutters shaped like teapots or teacups.

Cinnamon dough recipe:

2 cups of applesauce

3 cups of cinnamon (look for restaurant-sized containers at discount stores)

1 tablespoon of white glue

Prepare the dough and roll out a thick sheet. Cut shapes. Dry for about 2 hours at 200 degrees F. or allow to air-dry for several days. Baking them just prior to the party fills the room with a sweet cinnamon smell.

The following teapot (page 53) and teacup (page 55) patterns for garland were created by Catherine Archer-Wills. These also make great coloring pages.

www.Fun-With-Tea.com

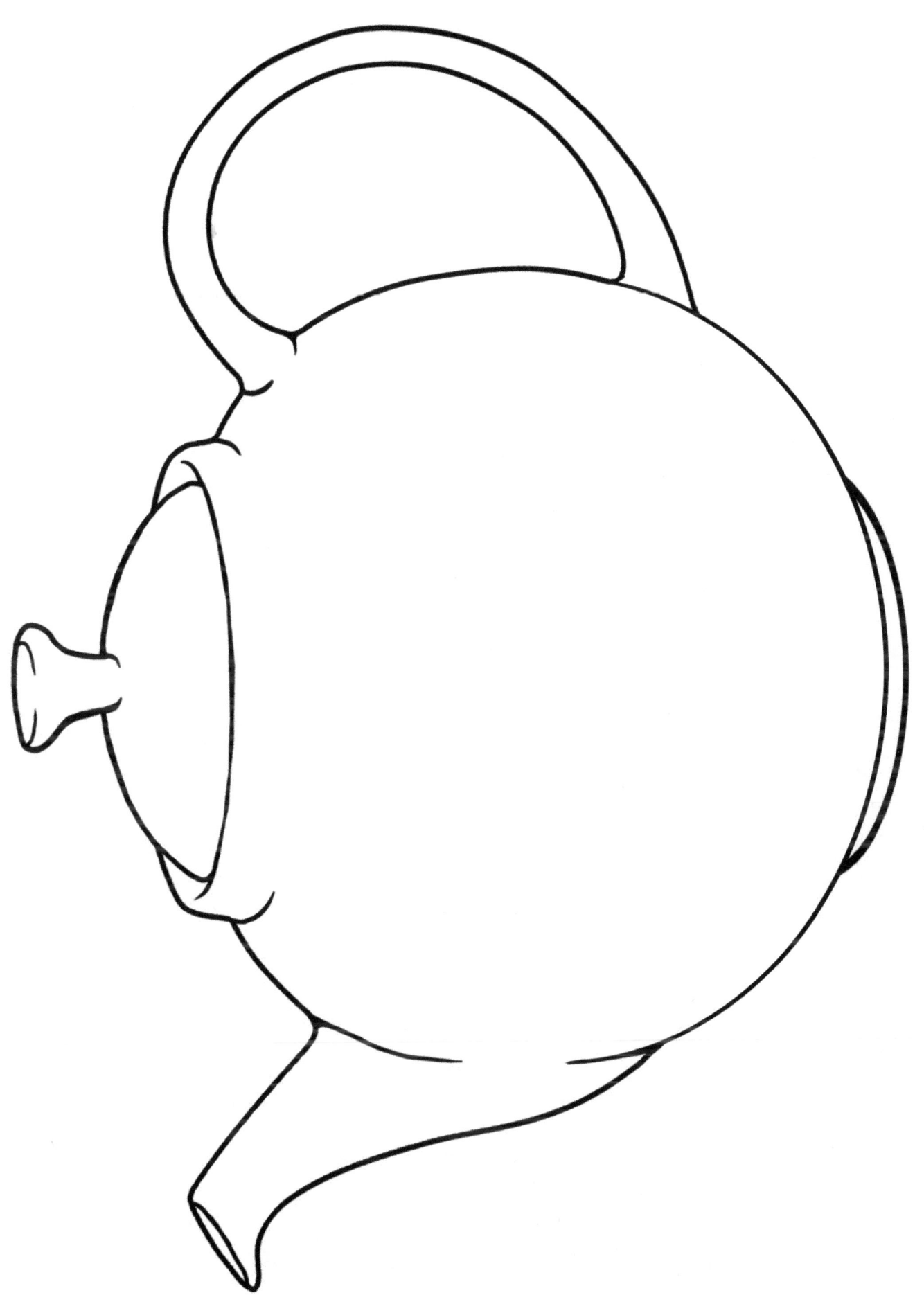

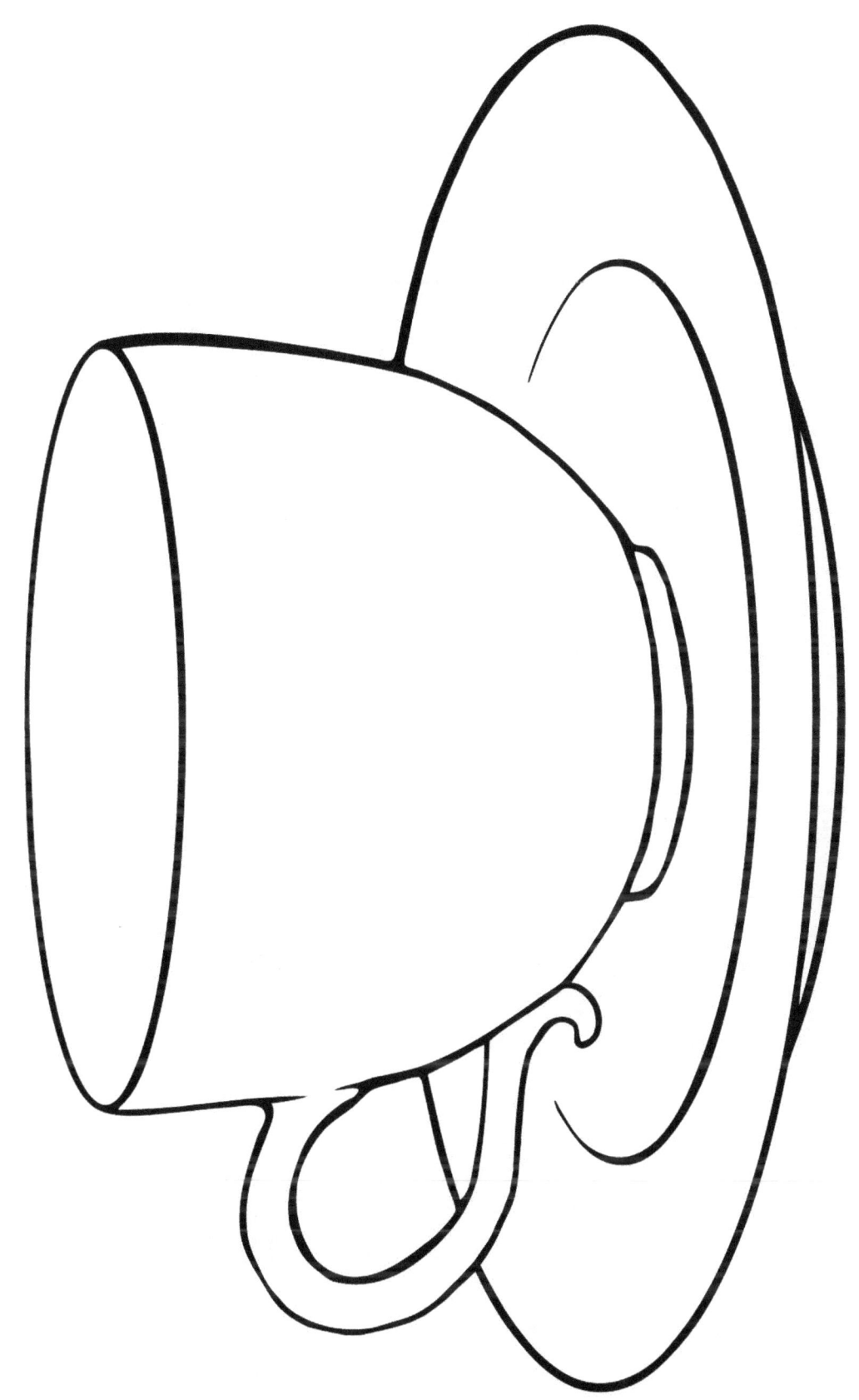

www.Fun-With-Tea.com

Teacup Place Cards

Pattern created by Lexxy Eve

These can be prepared in advance for your guests or can be a quick little craft project.

Cut along the solid lines. Fold on dashed lines. Glue the overlap.

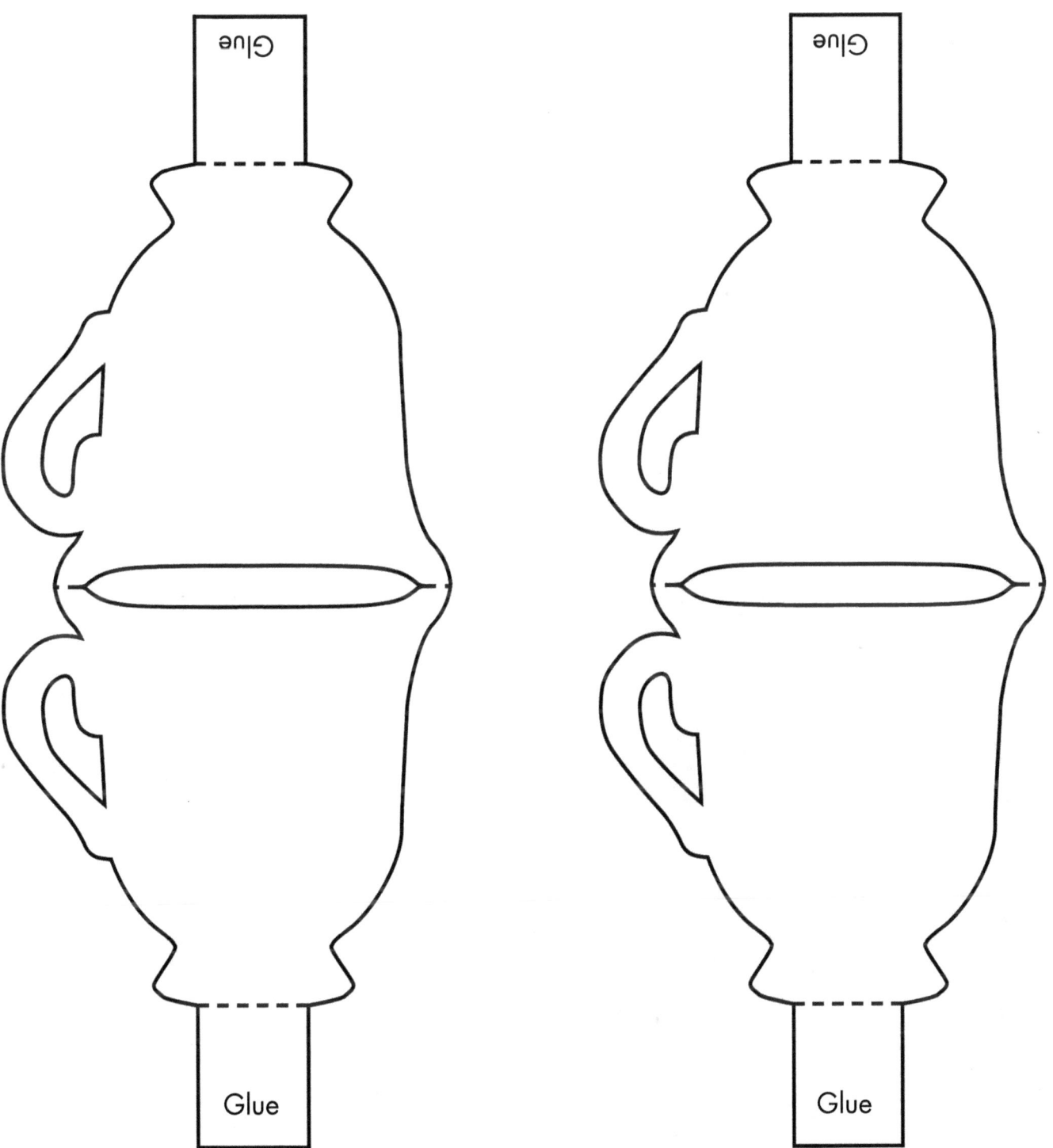

www.Fun-With-Tea.com

www.Fun-With-Tea.com

Teapot Party Favor Box

Pattern created by Lexxy Eve

This template will hold a small arrangement of flowers, a piece of homemade candy or a sample teabag of your own tea blend. It can double as a place card to identify each guest's seat.

Cut along the solid lines. Fold on dashed lines. Glue the overlap.

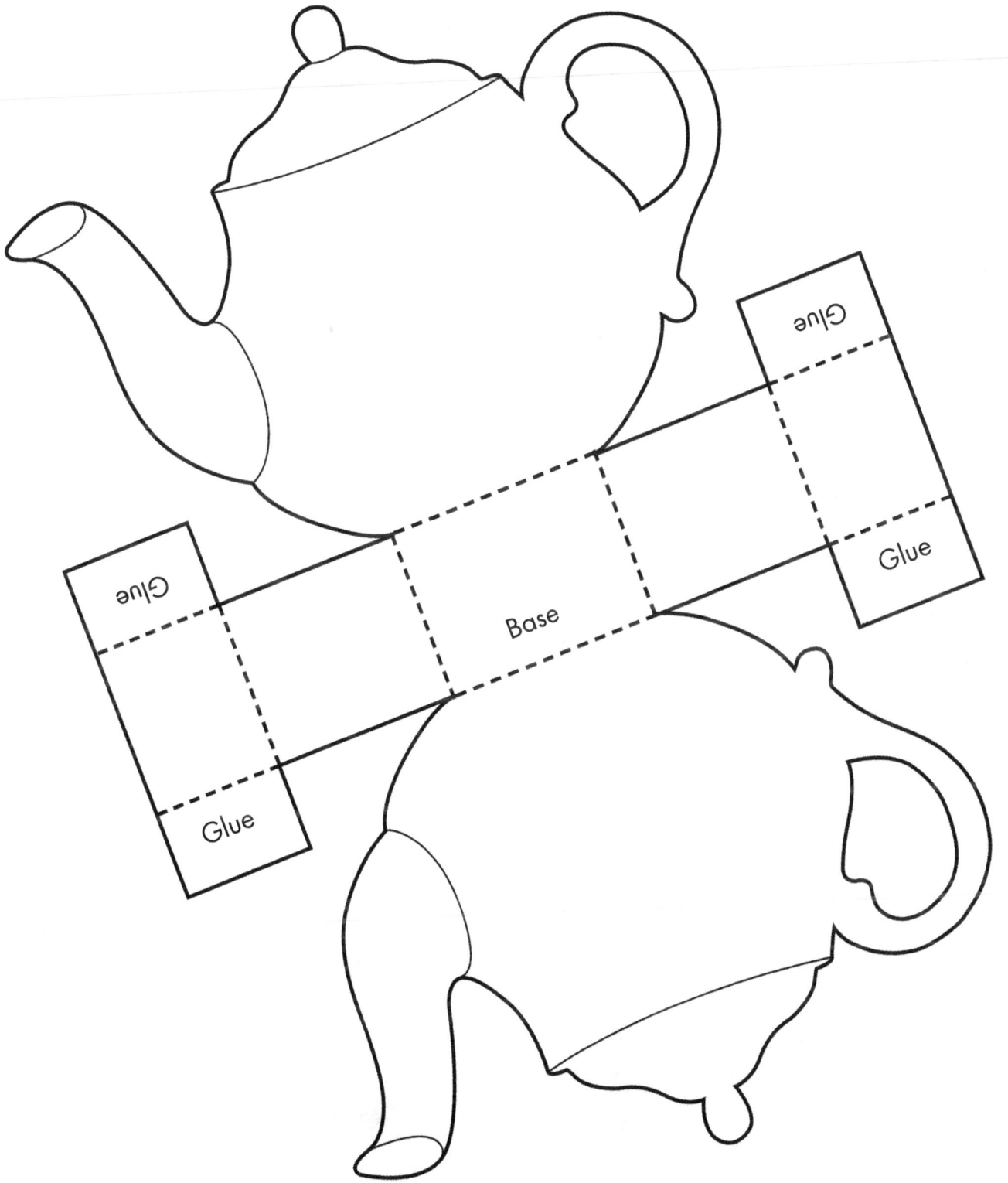

www.Fun-With-Tea.com

A Paper Teacup Party Decoration

This is a craft that can be used as a party activity for older children, a party decoration made in advance, or just something for a fun afternoon. One of the reasons we like it is because we've been able to recycle greeting cards, old file folders, cut-off ends of wallpaper and lots of sewing scraps.

What you need:

- Pattern follows the instruction
- Heavy paper or cardstock (like a Manila folder)
- Glue - a clear, quick-drying glue works best (Mod-Podge, Allene's Tacky Glue or a hot glue gun)
- Scissors, markers, crayons
- Other decorations such as glitter, lace, felt, colored tissue paper
- Clothes pins, paper clips or tape (options to help hold the cup while the glue dries)

Copy the pattern onto your paper:

If you remove the pattern from the book or download the PDF of the pattern from the website, you can use a copy machine to print it directly onto standard sized paper. It can easily be enlarged or reduced as well. One old-fashioned method is to either trace the pattern or use carbon paper (very old-fashioned method!) to transfer the design onto another sheet of paper.

Decorating:

Copying onto pre-printed paper like that available at scrapbooking craft shops is one quick way to make a quantity for a large event. If this is a craft project for children, have them decorate the cup pieces before cutting the paper.

Cutting & Gluing:

Cut out all the pieces and check that you see how they will fit together before gluing. There is a cut line indicated on the glue strip for the handle to make it easier to cut inside the small space.

The handle tab is glued to the overlap.

The two small circles are glued to the inside of the saucer and to the underside of the saucer to cover the snipped points.

The saucer: Snipping the lines in the base of the saucer that look like the spoke of a bicycle wheel help it sit flat. The two 1" circles are optional covers to hide these snipped points - inside where the teacup will be glued and the other and on the outside or underside (the bottom). Finish the saucer before gluing the teacup to it.

Plan to work slowly when gluing, allowing for enough time for glue to dry between each step.

The teacup: Be sure to glue the handle in place on the glue strip before gluing the teacup sides together. Hold it together until the glue sets or clip it together with a paperclip.

The final step is to put a ring of glue on the bottom of the teacup and position it in the center of the saucer, holding it in place while it dries.

Decorate:

There are hundreds of ways to decorate. In the sample photo on page 61, we've added felt inside the cup and lace on the outside in the space between the teacup and the saucer.

A Paper Teacup Party Decoration, *continued*

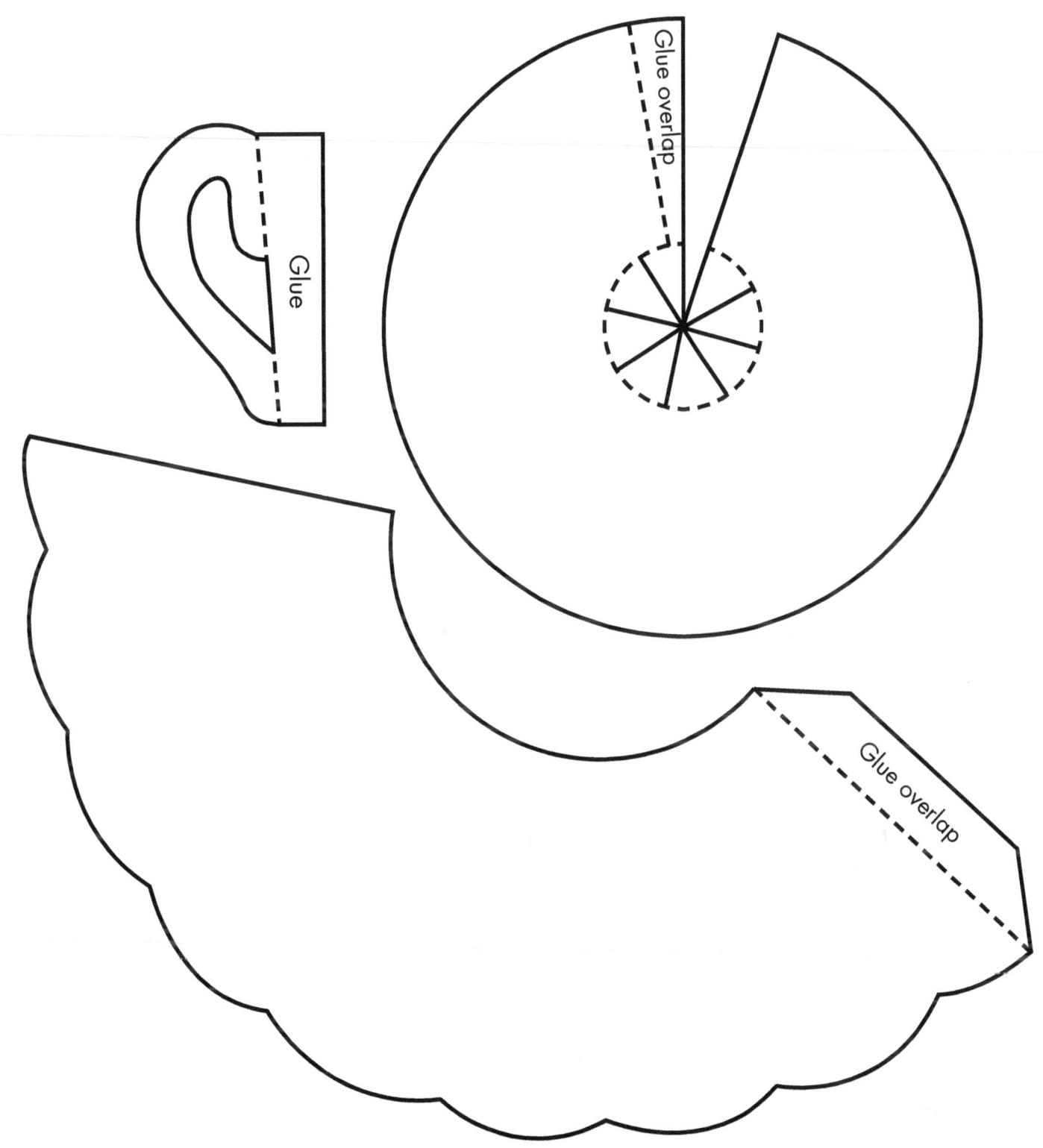

Website password: TSipFun4You

www.Fun-With-Tea.com

Teapot Chinese Paper Lantern

This quick project may not be a craft to do with a young child but it helps set the mood for a party for all ages. A single lantern can hang over the front door or over the table. A string of them can light an entire room.

What you need:

- A spherical Chinese paper lantern with the metal rings inside. A good quality one also has an additional wire frame piece to give tension to hold the shape. Others have a weight on the bottom so that it's pulled down to stay round. Our pattern was designed for a lamp with a 38" circumference at the largest point.

- Pattern for lid, spout, handle and optional base (next page)

- Cardstock or heavy paper

- A light source. This can be a low wattage bulb or a string of cool LED lights. Do not use cancles.

- Quick-drying glue that dries clear. (Mod Podge or a hot glue gun.)

- Clear tape to reinforce the cuts in the tissue paper

- Small craft knife with sharp, thin, pointed blade to cut small slits in the tissue paper

Cut your pattern pieces:

Cut one piece of each of the lid, spout and handle pattern pieces. If you want to use the scalloped base, you will need two. If you want the spout and handle to look thicker, cut two of each pattern piece and add a spacer between them. This could be an extra piece of folded paper or a thin piece of foam. Glue the flap of the lid under the opposite edge and hold it to dry. Fold the flaps all the way back so that the lid will sit on the top of the lamp.

Tip for adding glue:

The easiest way to add small drops of glue and then spread it is to use a paperclip where one side has been opened. The single wire holds the drop of glue and you have the rest of the paperclip to hold as you spread it.

Attaching the teapot spout and handle:

Locate and mark a slot between the wires where you want to attach your handle and spout. Gently cut slits for the tabs in the tissue paper with the tip of a sharp craft knife so that the tabs can slip inside and be folded over and glued back. Add glue and be ready to hold it in place until the glue has set. When completely dry, reinforce the cut area with clear tape.

Attaching the lid:

Glue your lid together with the flap underneath on the seam. Wait until it has dried before attaching it to the top of the lamp. Add glue to the flaps and position it on top of the lamp, holding it until the glue sets.

Attaching the base:

Our little scalloped edge is optional. But you do want to use it, adjust the length of the two pieces to fit the circumference of the bottom hole. Fold the flaps back, add glue and hold in place until the glue dries.

Lighting the lamp:

Chinese paper lanterns are almost always designed to be hung from a cord with a socket for a single light bulb. This system works with the addition of our teapot elements in just the same way. But we've also filled it with a small string of holiday lights that have a battery pack so they don't need to be plugged into an outlet.

Teapot Chinese Paper Lantern, *continued*

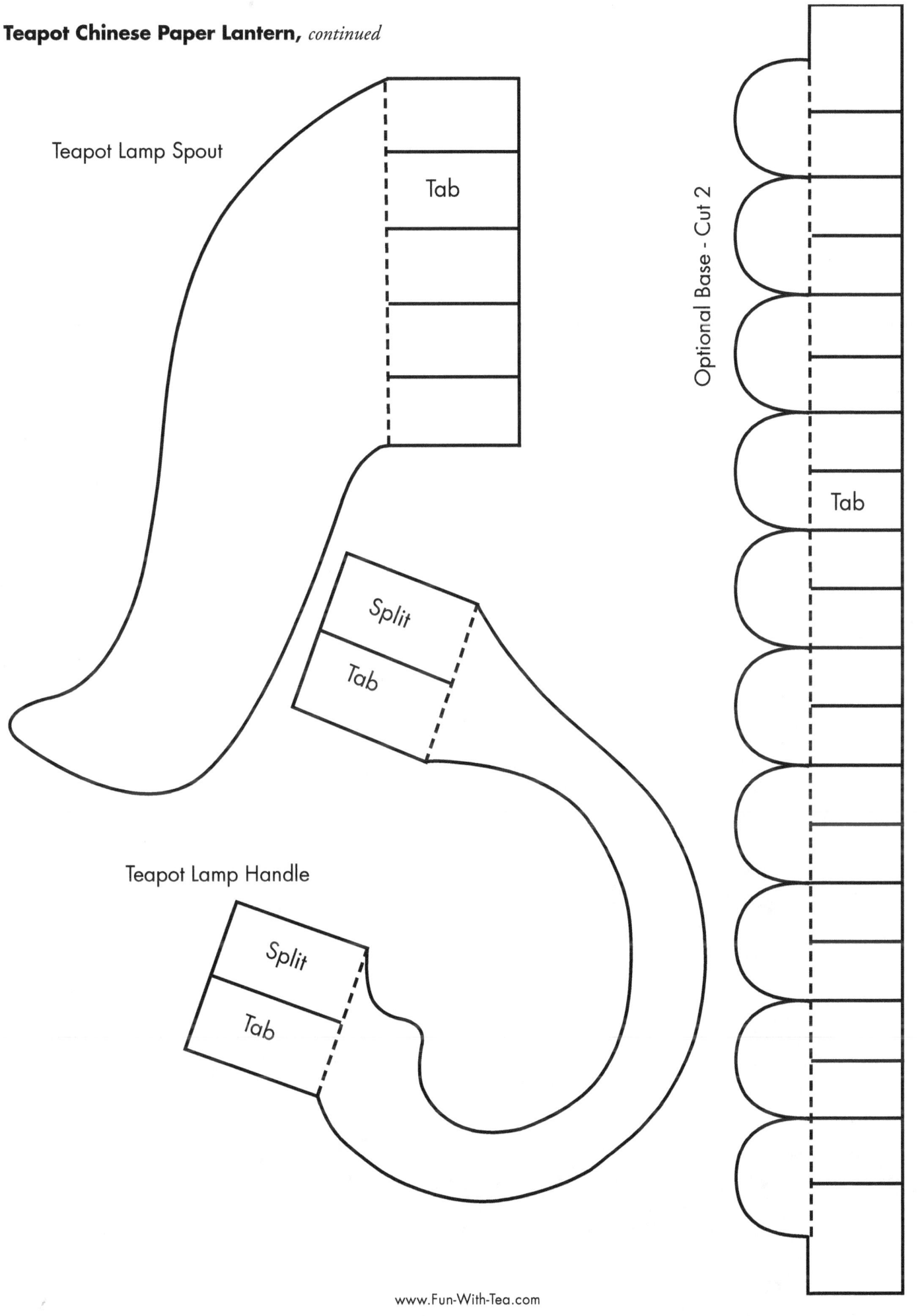

www.Fun-With-Tea.com

www.Fun-With-Tea.com

Teapot Chinese Paper Lantern, *continued*

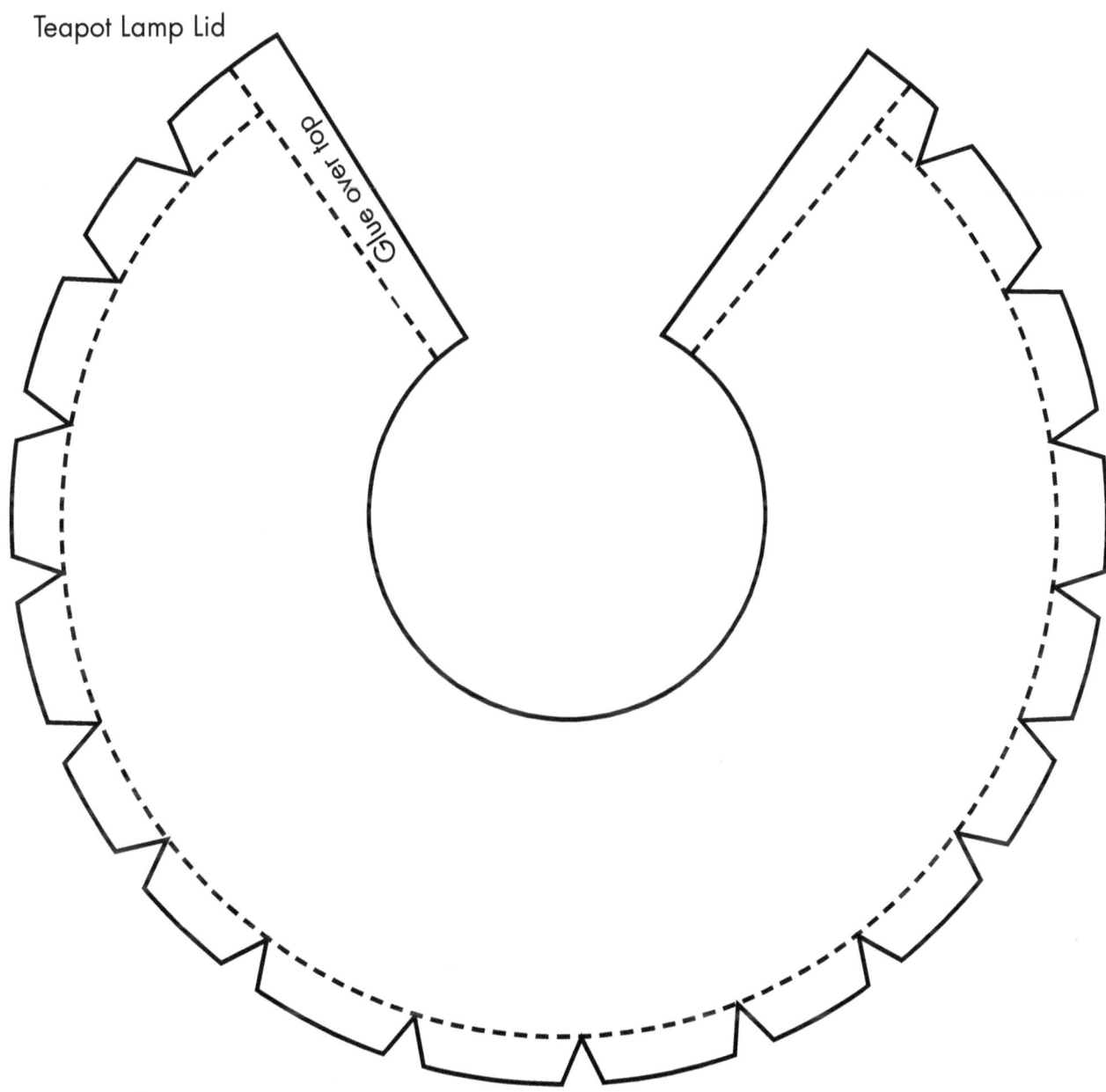

Teapot Lamp Lid

Glue over top

www.Fun-With-Tea.com

Extra-Large Papier Mâché Teapot & Teacup with Saucer

Papier mâché is a wonderful art medium for all ages. Layers of paper saturated with glue dry into a thick, hard surface that can be painted with bright colors. We recommend it here as a party decoration but also make it part of a game on page 73 at the end of this project.

What you may need:

- Paper—not glossy, preferably newsprint
- Glue (wallpaper paste, white glue, flour and water)
- Plastic drop-cloth
- Teapot & Teacup Forms: bowls, balls, balloons, rings, wire
- Saucer Form: Snow dish, circular serving tray
- Petroleum jelly
- Modeling clay
- Cardboard
- Thick Styrofoam (optional to carve pieces)
- Wire coat hanger (optional handle)
- Styrofoam wreath form in a size proportionate to your ball
- 30" of ½" - 1" thick rope (optional base rather than Styrofoam wreath form)
- 1 Ping-Pong ball
- Drying rack
- Utility knife
- Scissors
- Masking tape - or duct tape
- Hot glue gun (optional)
- Sandpaper - fine
- Acrylic paint
- Paint bushes
- Water
- Gloss varnish

Selecting & preparing forms:

Our large teapot and teacup were formed on a large exercise ball and the saucer was molded over a round snow saucer used to sit in when sliding down a hill. But you can use almost any size ball, bowl or plate to create your project. In some cases, you may opt to cover your ball with paper and leave it inside. Then it needs no additional preparation. If you want to remove the finished project from the form, first coat it with a thin covering of petroleum jelly. The project will slip off easily.

Choosing a glue:

- Wallpaper paste - Is easier on cleanup and dries rather quickly. It comes pre-mixed or in dry powder. In either case, add more water than recommended for wallpapering and dilute it to a thickness like cream.
- Flour & Water - Mix equal amounts of sifted flour and water. Blend until all lumps are gone. If it thickens as you work, mix in additional water. This takes a little longer to dry than wallpaper paste and takes more scrubbing to remove dried bits from skin.
- White Glue - Dilute regular white glue 50%.

Ripping strips:

The paper you use can be almost anything that does not have a glossy finish. It needs to be porous, like newspaper, to absorb the glue. It's helpful to alternate different papers for each layer. Using the comic pages is one choice. Tear strips 1-2" wide and 6-12" long. Adjust the size of your strips to make it easy for your child helper to manage.

Applying strips:

Moisten both sides of each strip with the glue mixture. Apply strips evenly. Overlap the edges slightly with all the strips going the same direction. (Alternate direction with each layer.) Allow 1-3 days for each layer to dry before adding another. When your form is thick enough, allow it to dry several additional days before painting. (See note about removing the ball below.)

Removing the ball:

If you are using a ball that you want to remove, consider the air release valve the bottom of the teapot and avoid covering the area around it. Make sure that you can see it. Leave the area around it light enough to cut away easily but don't deflate it until the teapot is thoroughly dry. When your teapot is sturdy, deflate the ball. Cut away enough of the thin paper to be able to pull the deflated ball out through the hole. Smooth the cut edge. Consider painting the inside of the teapot to seal the surface if you want it to last longer.

Teapot base:

The easiest base is a foam ring such as one used to make wreaths. Even if it has been used before, once it's covered with paper and glue, it will be very durable. Another option is to use a length of thick rope cut to fit the size of your teapot ball. Join the ends in a circle with masking tape. With either the rope or the wreath, wrap with several layers of glue-soaked paper. When both parts are ready, glue the base to the ball using a hot glue gun or strong white glue and let it dry.

Teapot handle:

The handle can be cut from a piece of Styrofoam or shaped with clothes hanger wire. After wrapping it with a thick layer of pasted strips and letting them dry completely, position the handle where you want it on the side of the teapot ball. A hot glue gun can help you hold it temporarily while you anchor it firmly with heavy tape like duct tape.

Extra-Large Papier Mâché Teapot & Teacup with Saucer, *continued*

Teapot spout:

We've provided a simple spout pattern that can be cut from a flat piece of cardboard. One of the easiest ways to fashion a spout is to glue pieces of Styrofoam to each side of the spout pattern and then carve the curves. Cover with a layer of glued strips and let dry completely. Attach it to the teapot ball just as you did the handle.

Teapot lid:

Mark the line on your teapot ball where you want the lid. Using the heavy tape or the hot glue gun, secure it to the ball. Using a Ping Pong ball for the top knob, flatten one side slightly or cut away a small bit and glue it to the top of the teapot ball.

Teacup:

When making the teacup, only cover half the ball. Be sure to use the petroleum jelly so that you can remove the cup. Add enough layers - drying between each one - to make it strong enough to support the handle.

As with the teapot, use a coat hanger or other stiff wire to make the "C" shape or cut a piece of flat Styrofoam. Wrap one end of the wire over the rim and tape it securely or cut the foam to fit the side of the teacup. Tape the bottom end near the base. Secure with a tape such as duct tape.

Saucer:

For the large saucer using the snow dish (round plastic used for sliding down a snowy hill) cover the surface you're using - inside or outside - with petroleum jelly. Apply strips as you're doing with the other pieces. When you've built up enough layers, remove it from the form and allow it to dry completely. Then paint and finish with gloss sealer.

Final layers of *papier mâché*:

When all the attachments are firmly in place, continue applying layers of paper strips being careful to apply evenly and to alternate the direction of the strips between layers. Let dry 2-3 days between layers. Continue until you've built up the surface so that it looks like one piece. Let dry 4-5 days before painting.

Finishing:

Deflate and remove the inside exercise ball if desired. Lightly sand the outer surface to reduce the lines of the paper. Paint with a base coat of paint. You might consider a coat of primer that has better "stick" than some other paints. The base coat will probably require two coats for good coverage. Follow directions on the paint products for drying times.

Decorating:

Paint with colorful acrylic paints or tempera paint. Decorations can also be added like decoupage. Allow all decorations to dry thoroughly. Consider sealing it with a gloss varnish or sealer.

Timing:

This project can take 2 weeks to a month to finish due to the drying times. This varies greatly with the thickness of paper and glue as well as weather conditions - whether you live in a very dry climate or humid one. If your *papier mâché* teaware will be used for a special event, be sure to allow enough time for at least 5 layers of glued strips to dry and then a few extra days for painting and adding the clear sealer if needed.

Tea Party Game For Young Children: "How Does The Elephant Drink His Tea"

This is a simple game for improvisation and silly fun. Encourage children to use their imaginations and to be good hosts, including everyone, no matter how different they may be. The reason we usually begin with the elephant is that he has to deal with his large size and most children have fun trying to use an arm as a pretend trunk to drink tea from the teacup. Other fun animals are slithery snakes who don't have hands to hold a teacup properly, chickens who only have a little beak, puppy dogs who lap the tea with their tongues but may wag their tails so much they knock over the dishes, spiders (think of Charlotte), pigs (think of Wilbur) and bulls (what about Ferdinand?).

Create a set of cards with pictures and/or words for animals that are familiar to the children.

The choice of animals should be ones that are easy to act out.

Ask each child to draw a card and then sit in a circle around the teacup.

The adult then asks, "How does the Elephant (or other animal) drink his tea?"

The child with that card acts out the part of the animal and imagines how they might behave at a tea party.

As each new "animal" comes to the party, the children are encouraged to remain in character and welcome the new guest to tea.

One child may be designated as the host and would try to figure out who should sit next to each other and what kind of snack each animal would want with their tea.

Using animals from your child's storybooks adds an additional level of fun.

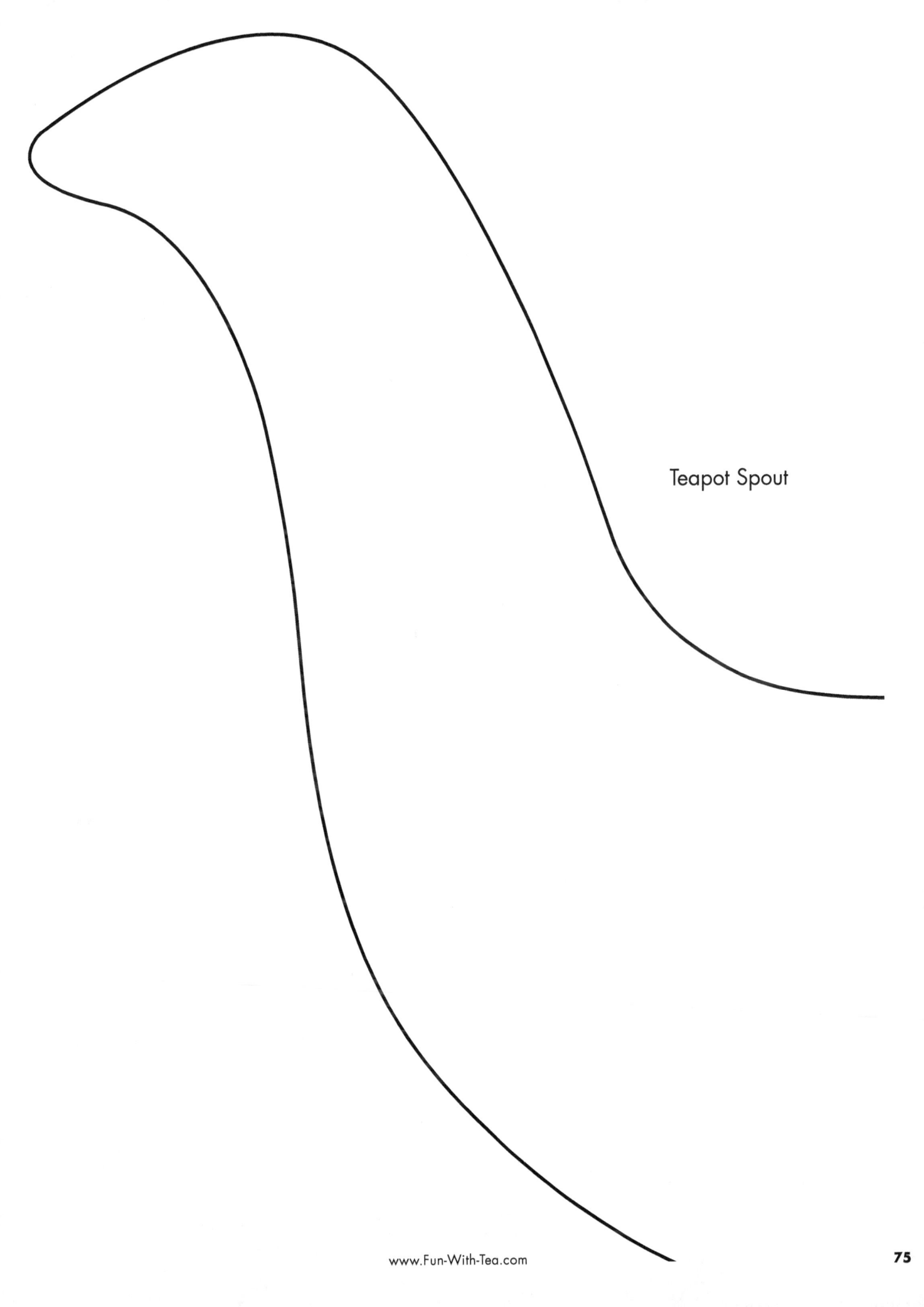

Teapot Spout

Website password: TSipFun4You

www.Fun-With-Tea.com

Musical Teacup Games

These games are not just for children. Adults also enjoy these tea-themed variations of classic party games. For some of these options, you may want to use our teacup crafts to create non-breakable teaware.

Version 1: Ring Around The Table - Sing-Along Fun

To the tune of "Ring Around The Rosie" sing the tea party lyrics:

> *Ring around the table, set with pretty teacups.*
> *Choose one. Choose one. It's time for tea.*

The guests circle around the table. Each guest holds his/her own place card or name tag. Repeat the song three or more times, long enough for everyone to walk slowly around the table and spot a favorite teacup or place setting. As the circle continues, guests can set their names at the chosen place setting but continue walking and singing. With younger children or those who might have difficulty making a decision, have an adult walk with them and encourage the choice of where to sit - especially if it's important for them to sit together.

Note: This may not be a good choice for a large or rowdy group.

Version 2: Pass The Teacup

Guests are seated in a circle and all but one has an unbreakable teacup to pass around. Like musical chairs, when the music begins, guests pass the cups in the designated direction until the music stops. Then the guest who doesn't have a cup leaves the circle and one cup is removed. The game continues until there is a final winner. A twist on this game is that your "prizes" might be that the one eliminated from the game goes to a table of teacups and chooses the one they will use for the party and takes it to their place at the table.

Version 2.1

A variation on "Pass The Teacup" is to have the teacups the guests will be using wrapped in gift boxes. Then, one box is passed around the circle. When the music stops, the person holding that box leaves the circle with their teacup. They are directed to the table where they open the box and choose their place at the table. The game continues until everyone has a box and the guests are all seated, ready to have their tea poured. This works best when the teacups are gifts will be taken home. The empty boxes can be slipped under the guests' chairs during the meal and then used to wrap their teacup to take home.

Version 3: Find your Seat

For a calmer game that works better with a larger or more active group, a teacup filled with numbered slips of paper is passed around. Everyone draws a number. The number matches a place setting at the table. Children can be seated as each number is drawn.

Version 4: Everybody Sings

A single teacup holds strips of paper on which the lines of familiar friendship songs are written. Everyone draws one or two lines to sing. No none is able know the order in which everyone else will sing - they only know their part.

Begin by singing in unison. On the second (or third time through the song) the guests will "solo" their part - the lines that are on their slips of paper. Some suggestions are: the traditional Girl Scout song, "Make New Friends", "The More We Get Together", Raffi's "The Sharing Song", James Taylor's "You've Got A Friend", The Beatles, "With A Little Help From My Friends".

Version 5: Balancing Teacups

Using an unbreakable teacup such as the fabric or paper examples we've included in other sections of Fun With Tea, set up relay races in which the teacup is balanced on the top of the guests' heads.

Version 6: How Does The Elephant Drink His Tea?

Create a set of cards with pictures and/or words for animals that are familiar to the group and easy to pantomime. Ask each guest to draw a card and then sit in a circle. The leader asks, "How does the Elephant (or other animal) drink his tea?" The child with that card acts out the part of the animal and imagines how they might behave at a tea party. The children are encouraged to remain in character and welcome the new guest to tea.

If the theme of the tea party is about the animals, place settings can be coordinated with the animal personalities. After the game, everyone finds his or her seat at the table. You consider creating your menu items to match your animal theme. It could be something as simple as peanuts for the elephant or bananas for the monkey. Or you could cut out, decorated sugar cookies in the shapes of the animals.

(This game is also described with the "Papier mâché Teapot", page 73.)

Version 7: Mad Lib Game

Teacups hold slips of paper with nouns, verbs, adjectives, adverbs and names - one teacup for each category - to fill in the "Teatime Mad Lib" (next page - #79, and #80). It can be read aloud as the guests pull the slips from the teacups.

"I'm A Little Teapot" Easy Mad Lib

You may want to copy the list of questions so the people playing don't know how the answers to the clues will be used. The responses will be much more random and more fun when read.

Clues:

1. A noun - _____

2. An adjective - describe your noun _____

3. An adjective - describe your noun _____

4. A noun - _____

5. A noun - _____

6. A feeling - _____

7. A verb - _____

8. A verb - _____

9. A verb - _____

I'm a little [#1 *noun*], [#2 *adjective*] and [#3 *adjective*]
Here is my [#4 *noun*]. Here is my [#5 *noun*].
When I get all [#6 *feeling*] hear me [#7 *verb*].
Just [#8 *verb*] me over and [#9 *verb*].

"I'm A Little Teapot" Easy Mad Lib

Tea Party Mad Lib Clues

When everyone is finished, have one person read the story using clues from the list above. A Mad Lib can be done by one person, by teams or with different party guests each contributing one or more answer to complete the story.

Fill in as many of the clues as possible to create the story. You may want to work in teams.

1. A number more than twice your age _____
2. Name of a wild animal _____
3. Reason for having a tea party _____
4. A kind of a fairy tale character _____
5. Name of a cartoon character _____
6. Name of a super hero _____
7. Name of the author of a classic children's book _____
8. Name of one of the other guests at the party _____
9. Name of a flower _____
10. Name of a color _____
11. Your favorite food _____
12. List two tea party foods _____ & _____
13. Name of a flavor of tea _____
14. Repeat the name of cartoon character in #5 _____
15. A toy or game set played with outside _____
16. Repeat the name of the super hero in #6 _____
17. Something very large found in nature _____
18. Repeat the name of the author in #7 _____
19. Title of your favorite children's book _____
20. Name of a children's song _____
21. Repeat #8 - name of the other guest _____
22. A good feeling _____
23. A fun place to go _____
24. A large vehicle _____
25. An adjective _____

Tea Party Mad Lib

Once upon a time, about [#1   number more than twice your age   ] years ago, Mathilde [#2   name of a wild animal   ] wanted to give a [#3 kind of party] tea party for Alissa, a [#4 a kind fairy tale character]. Mathilde sent invitations to four guests, [#5 a cartoon character] , [#6 a super hero] , [#7   author of a children's book   ] and [#8 name of one of the other guests attending your party] who all promised bring something special. Mathilde decorated the party room with [#9 kind of flowers] and [#10 color] streamer and balloons. The table was set with trays of [#11 favorite tea party food] and [#12 two other - party foods] and Mathilde had made her favorite tea, [#13 kind of tea].

[#14 Repeat #5 the cartoon character] brought a [#15 an outside toy or game set] so they could all play outside before the party and [#16 repeat #6 name of the super hero] brought [#17 something rare and unusual from nature] and let everyone touch it carefully.
[#18 Repeat #7 the children's author] brought [#19 title of a book to read when they went inside]. Best thing of all was the song, [#20 name of a song] that [#21 Repeat #8 name of the party guest] taught them. Every detail made the party lots of fun and very special.

Mathilde felt so [#22 a good feeling] that she didn't want the party to end. She suggested that they all go to [#23 a fun place to go]. Everyone got into the [#24 name of a large vehicle] and continued to share a very [#25 adjective] happy day.

Teapot People Coloring Pages

Created by Alyssa Baker

We've included a group of teapot people coloring pages just for a little fun. Color them as they are in the book, copy them on a copier from the book and save your original page or download copies from our website: www.Fun-With-Tea.com using your member access password,

TSipFun4You.

While you're there, check out some of the other teatime activities and new things we have for you.

www.Fun-With-Tea.com

www.Fun-With-Tea.com

www.Fun-With-Tea.com

Section 4

Fun With Tea Party Recipes

These recipes are examples of ways in which simple ingredients can be adapted to fit a party theme. Our selection includes seasonal party themes, a fairy tea party and the traditional favorites.

Teapot cakes may take a lot of time to bake and decorate, but, of course, that's the real fun. At the very least, they can help adults share the fun of cooking with young children. Playtime in the kitchen also teaches many important life skills.

Recipes In This Section:

Spring: Strawberry Flowers	92
Spring: Matcha Mint Leaf Cookies	93
Summer: Cambric Tea Ice Cream In A Bag	94
Fall: Apple Pie Tea	95
Winter: Snowflake Cinnamon Toast	96
Fairy Flower Bread & Crystallized Violets	97
Bas-Relief Teapot Cake	98
3-D Teapot Cake	100
Homemade Fondant	102
Lemon Curd & Devonshire Cream	103
Mandarin Orange Scones	104

Strawberry Flowers

Great for a Spring Tea Party Theme! The Strawberry Flowers are fun to serve with the Matcha Mint Cookies if they are rolled and cut into leaf shapes then substituted for the sprigs of mint in the Strawberry Flower Recipe.

This recipe is written to makes 4 servings. We suggest serving 2-3 small flowers per person if they are used as one of the main foods or just one flower per plate if it is a decoration. Smaller strawberries usually make prettier flowers.

Ingredients:

- 2 teaspoons honey
- ¼ cup softened cream cheese
- 12 small ripe strawberries
- 12 large fresh blueberries
- ¼ cup flavored yogurt
- 12 sprigs of fresh mint leaves
- 2 Tablespoons sunflower seeds

Directions:

Wash the strawberries and blueberries. Let them dry on paper towels.

Soften the cream cheese and honey and stir together until smooth and creamy. Form the cream cheese into 12 small balls that will be the center of the flower. Use them to secure the cut strawberries to a plate and to hold the mint leaves in place under the strawberries. Arrange them on the plate so that the strawberries are about 1" apart.

Cut the strawberries top-to-bottom in thin wedges. Arrange them in a circle around the cream cheese centers. Depending on the size of the strawberry, you might be able to cut 4 - 8 "petals".

Add a small dollop of yogurt - about 1 teaspoon - into the center of each one. Then top the yogurt with one of the whole blueberries and a sprinkle of sunflower seeds.

Decorate with small sprigs of mint leaves under each strawberry by sticking the stem into the ball of cream cheese. Serve immediately.

Option:

Use the Matcha Mint Cookie recipe to roll out and cut leaf shapes. Serve these with the strawberry flowers instead of fresh mint to represent the leaves.

Matcha Mint Cookies

These slightly sweet cookies, when cut in a leaf shape, represent the fresh tea leaf and are a delight at any kind of tea party.

Makes approximately 36 cookies.

Ingredients:

1½ cups confectioner's sugar
1 cup butter, softened
2 teaspoon dried, crushed mint
2 cups all-purpose flour
2 Tablespoons Matcha tea
1 egg
1 teaspoon almond extract
Baking parchment paper

Directions:

Preheat the oven to 350 º F.
Line a baking pan with parchment paper.

Cream the butter in a large mixing bowl. Gradually add the powdered sugar to the creamed butter until well blended. Add the egg and mix thoroughly. Add almond extract, matcha powder and mint. Add the flour gradually and incorporate it thoroughly. The batter will be stiff.

Chill in the refrigerator until firm, one hour or overnight. Dough can be formed into small, walnut-sized balls and placed on the parchment-lined baking pan. They will flatten slightly as they bake.

The cookie dough can also be rolled on a lightly floured surface and then cut into shapes like the suggestions made in the Strawberry Flowers recipe.

The parchment paper helps the backs of the cookies brown evenly but not burn. Cookies can also be baked on a lightly greased surface.

Bake for 12-15 minutes, until slightly golden around the edges.

More About Matcha:

Matcha Tea is powdered green tea used in the traditional Japanese tea ceremony, Chanoyu. It is made by grinding the entire leaf and a sometimes a very small bit of stem into a fine powder. Since the entire leaf is consumed rather than just infused in hot water, it has a significantly higher antioxidant value and is one of the healthiest teas to drink and to use in cooking. The small amount used for this recipe gives the cookies a nice green color without adding additional food dye. Many different grades are now available and the cooking grade is much less expensive than the ceremonial grade.

Cambric Tea Ice Cream In A Bag

The highlights of old fashioned family gatherings may have been taking a turn cranking the ice cream churn to make your own frosty treat. It's delicious to serve at tea parties but also fun to share as an activity. Everyone can make their own flavor and share with a tasting of the sweet results.

Ingredients:

- ¾ cup boiling water
- 2 teabags, your favorite brand of black tea
- 1 cup half-and-half
- 3 Tablespoons sugar
- 4 Tablespoons evaporated milk
- 4 cups crushed ice
- ¾ cup rock salt
- 2 large, heavy-duty zip-closure baggies

Directions:

Brew the double-strength tea by using two teabags in slightly less water than you would usually use. Allow this to cool slightly before adding it to the rest of the ingredients in one of the zip-closure bags. (Consider using the heavy-duty kind with two closure strips to insure it won't leak while you're mixing the ice cream.)

When closing the bag, try to remove as much of the air as possible. You might want to stabilize the bag of liquid ingredients by nesting it into a large bowl while closing the seal.

Fill the second bag with the ice and rock salt. Add the bag with your tea and milk mixture. Press the air out of the bag of ice and salt. Shake and agitate the bag gently for about 10-15 minutes until you can feel the mixture become thick and firm - being careful not to open the seals on the two bags. Allow it to sit in the bag of ice until ready to serve - or store it in the freezer.

Serving your Cambric Tea Ice Cream:

Open your outer bag carefully over the sink. Rinse the salt from the inner bag before opening. Serve with fresh berries or other favorite toppings.

Other tasty tea flavors:

- Chai and chai blends
- Berry and apple flavors and blends
- Chocolate teas and blends
- Caramel-flavored tea blends
- Matcha

Apple Pie Tea

Fall tea parties can feature the fruits of the season and the fun of preserving the harvest.
Makes 5 - 6 servings

Tea Ingredients:

- 1 can apple pie filling (21 oz)
- 1 cup milk
- 4 cups brewed Rooibos tea
- 1 cup apple cider

Topping Ingredients:

The topping is optional but adds to the festivities.

- 1 teaspoon apple pie spice
- 1 cup whipping cream
- 2 teaspoons apple cider

Topping Directions:

Prepare the topping by whipping the cream with electric mixer or hand whisk until it forms peaks. Mix in 2 teaspoons of the apple cider and the teaspoon of apple pie spice. Keep it chilled in the refrigerator until the hot drink is ready to serve.

Tea Directions:

Brew the cup of Rooibos tea (plain or flavored). Let it cool slightly. Blend the apple pie filling in a blender on a low speed until smooth and creamy. Gradually add the milk, tea and apple juice. Pour the mixture into a saucepan and heat over low heat until steamy but not boiling. Serve this thick and creamy tea in teacups or mugs. Add the topping (if desired) and serve immediately.

Homemade Apple Pie Filling Option:

- 4 Granny Smith or Pippin Apples
- 2 Tablespoons butter
- ¼ cup water
- ½ cup brown sugar
- 1 teaspoon cinnamon

Directions:

Peel, core and slice the apples. Saute in the butter for 10 minutes. Stir in brown sugar, cinnamon and water. Simmer until the apples are soft and begin to break apart. Then, blend this with the Rooibos tea -- or other favorite tea -- as described in the Apple Pie Tea recipe above.

Snowflake Cinnamon Toast

This is usually a breakfast recipe but is also fun for lunch or afternoon tea. It's an easy and inexpensive idea for a winter tea party theme.

Serves 4

Ingredients:

- 4 slices of bread
- 1 stick of butter, melted (or ½ cup butter substitute, melted)
- 1 cup granulated sugar
- 2 Tablespoons ground cinnamon
- ½ cup powdered sugar
- A Snowflake stencil or other decoration of your choice
- 2 cups applesauce

Directions:

Preheat your broiler.

Blend the cinnamon and sugar. Melt the butter. Place the bread on a flat baking sheet. It helps prevent burning and makes cleanup easier to line the baking pan with parchment. With a pastry brush, coat one side of the bread with the melted butter. Broil until very lightly browned. Remove from the broiler and turn the bread.

Warm the applesauce while the bread is broiling.

Coat the other side with melted butter.

Sprinkle the surface of the bread with a generous coating of the cinnamon-sugar mixture. Return to the broiler but watch carefully. The sugar will melt into the butter and bubble, forming a crusty sugar topping for the cinnamon toast. While the toast is broiling, add powdered sugar to a sifter. Remove toast from the oven and lay the stencil(s) on top of each piece. Then dust with powdered sugar while the toast is still warm. Serve with warm applesauce.

Activity with children:

Cutting paper snowflakes has been a traditional winter craft for generations. An older child can make his/her own snowflake decoration by folding and cutting the paper. A younger child may need assistance.

Fold the paper in half, then quarters. Then, bringing the two closed sides together, fold it into eights so that it creates a triangle. Cut notches on the two sides that, when unfolded, look like a snowflake.

Lay the cut pattern flat on the Cinnamon Toast and dust with the powdered sugar so that you make a snowflake. Remember, no two snowflakes are ever alike!

Fairy Flower Bread

Fairy tea parties make a wonderful dress-up theme.
This delicate bread can be served like open-faced sandwiches with fresh berries.

Serves 15-20

Ingredients:

- 1 cup cake flour
- ½ teaspoon salt
- 8 egg whites, chilled
- Grated peeling from one lemon
- 1½ teaspoon cream of tartar
- ½ cup sugar
- 1 Tablespoon lemon juice
- 2 cups fresh edible flower petals

Prepare flower petals:

Flower petals can be all one kind of flower or a combination of edible blossoms and herbs: roses, day lilies, violets, calendula and mint are a few suggestions. Separate the flower petals. Wash the flowers in cold water. Strain and dry completely on a clean towel. Chop lightly for smaller particles that cut more easily when slicing. Set aside.

Prepare cake batter:

Preheat oven to 350 ºF. Grate the lemon peel and squeeze the juice. Sift flour before measuring. Then sift together flour and sugar. Set aside. Beat the chilled egg whites until foamy and starting to peak. Then add salt and cream of tartar. Continue beating until the peaks are stiff. Add lemon peel and lemon juice. Using a spatula, slowly fold the dry ingredients into the egg whites and flower petals. Transfer to an un-greased bread pan and bake until the top is browned and it bounces back when touched, about 30 minutes. Do not attempt to slice the bread until it is completely cool.

Optional: Prepare a recipe of the Crystallized Violets and decorate.

Crystallized Violets

Ingredients:

- 1 cup violets
- 1 cup superfine sugar
- ½ teaspoon warm water
- 1 egg white
- Baking parchment

Directions:

Preheat oven to 200° F. Wash the violets thoroughly and allow them to dry on paper towel. Whip the egg white and ½ teaspoon warm water until frothy. Dip the flowers into the egg white and then into the sugar. Place them on a baking sheet lined with parchment. Let the flowers dry in the 200° oven for 1 hour with the oven door slightly open. Turn off the oven, close the door and allow the heat of the oven to continue a slow drying.

Bas-Relief Teapot Cake

Bas-Relief is the term for sculpture that usually hangs on the wall so the back side is flat. But the front has been carved with detail. With this cake, instead of trying to make the teapot stand up, a large layer cake serves as the background for a half of a teapot. This is easer to construct and decorate. It also serves more people, requiring the equivalent of two standard cake recipes to make.

When pricing a professionally decorated teapot cake at a local bakery it was surprising to hear that it will be between $200-$300. Work of art that it is, this is a bit out of most tea party budgets so we created a more affordable option that is also a great family project. Even little fingers can help with mixing and decorating.

Serves 16-20

What you need:

- Ingredients to prepare a double batch of your favorite cake mix or recipe
- One 9" x 13" rectangular baking pan
- One 8" round baking pan
- One side of the sphere baking set
- Your favorite frosting recipe, doubled if you want to decorate with color
- Food dye for frosting if desired
- Edible decorations - fondant, candies, sprinkles, colored sugars, crystalized violets, etc.

Baking your cakes:

Prepare both batches of your cake mix or cake recipe - enough to bake one 9" x 13" and one half-sphere plus one 8" round layer. Follow the directions on the box or instructions provided with your recipe. Follow the directions for preparing baking pans and bake at the recommended temperature.

Remove from pans. Allow the layers to cool completely before cutting or assembling.

The teapot base, spout, handle and lid:

Once it has cooled completely and is a little firmer, slice the 8" round, flat layer cake into two thin layers. From this, cut a "C" shape for the handle and a small arch for the base. Another arch can be cut for the lid. Then, one of the small pieces can be shaped into a spout.

Note: In our photo, we showed another option, using candies to form a thin handle. This was a little easier for beginner cake decorators (like our volunteer team).

Frosting:

Prepare the double batch of frosting. Use two small dollops to anchor the 9" x 13" cake to a large caterer's cake cardboard or large platter and cover with frosting. Center the full circle in the middle of the rectangle and press it lightly into the frosting. Line up the handle, lid and spout, pressing a dollop of frosting where each one attaches to the main round layer. Cover the entire teapot form with frosting.

Decorating:

There are hundreds of ways to decorate your Teapot Cake. The simplest is to have two different colors of frosting with some contrast so that the teapot is obvious. Using cake decorating tools, an outline can be added where the teapot sits on the rectangular base. Lines can also be made with red licorice strings. Decorations can be candies or edible flowers. You might also consider using fondant (page 102) to form a flat version of the lid, handle and spout.

3-D Teapot Cake

Assembling this little teapot cake requires a bit of patience and time for the frosting to cement the pieces together before moving to the next steps. Various baking cookware specialists offer a 3-D sphere cake pan. This is a two-part aluminum pan that includes two stabilizing rings in which each half sits while baking. The addition of a lid, spout, handle and base transform it into your special teapot.

Serves 6-8

What you need:

- Ingredients to prepare your favorite cake
- A batch of your favorite frosting
- Butter or margarine and a bit of flour for dusting the pan
- A sphere baking pan set with stabilizing rings
- 3 bamboo skewers
- 4 wooden toothpicks
- A large, thick and well-cooled sugar cookie (better if it's 1-2 days old and less crumbly)
- Pointy-ended sugar cone ice cream cone
- Cardboard cut in the spout pattern and decorated.
- Gum ball for the knob on the top of the lid
- Long tube - about 9" - of red or other colored licorice for the handle
- Long licorice string to define the teapot lid
- Candies or sprinkles to decorate

Baking your cake:

Preheat your oven to 350° Fahrenheit or the recommended temperature for your recipe. Prepare the pans. Prepare the batter for your cake. Fill the pans just over half full and in equal amounts.

(Commercial cake mixes usually fill both pans adequately.) While your cakes are baking, prepare your frosting, spout, handle and lid. Loosen the cakes from the pans. If there is overrun on the two sphere halves, then trim the cakes level with the brim with a serrated bread knife. Remove the cakes and cool completely. While the cakes are cooling, prepare your frosting recipe.

Creating your foundation:

Use a dollop of frosting to anchor the sugar cookie to the serving plate. Press firmly and set it in a cool place to harden until you're ready to assemble your teapot cake.

Handle, Spout and Lid:

There are many creative ways to create spouts and handles. The options suggested here are a pointed sugar cone ice cream cone for a spout and a thick licorice stick for a handle.

To form the spout, score the part of the cone that you want to break away with a small, serrated knife. This makes it easier to break away the brittle cone into your desired size and shape. The handle is the final piece. Push two toothpicks into each end of the licorice vine. It will form a "C", when you stick the two ends into the finished cake.

Assembling your teapot cake:

When the cake halves are completely cool, "de-crumb" the surface and coat with a thin layer of frosting to seal the surface. Let set 10-15 minutes.

Bottom layer: Shave a thin slice off the rounded dome top of the layer you'll use as the bottom layer to create a flat side so the cake will be stable. Add a dollop of frosting to the top of the cookie and seat the cut surface of the bottom half of the cake on top of the cookie. Stand the 2 bamboo skewers through the bottom half, poking into the cookie base. Allow this next step to set up about 15-20 minutes.

Top layer: Slice off a section of the rounded dome of the top layer to use as a lid and set it aside.

Remove the skewers long enough to frost the flat center surface. Place the top half of the cake on the bottom to complete the sphere. Secure with the 2 skewers - pushing the points into the cookie. Let it set another 15-20 minutes until firm.

Frost the sphere and let it set about 15 minutes. When the frosting on the cake has hardened, cut out a small, half-circle divot where the spout will be inserted.

Frost the spout - adding extra into the place it will be inserted in the cake. Secure it with the third skewer through the spout, pushed into the cake until the frosting has hardened.

Add the handle, poking the toothpicks into the cake so that about 1/4" of the ends of the licorice are buried under the frosting.

Remove the skewers and add a layer of frosting to the top of the cake to give the lid a little lift. Then settle the lid gently in place

Decorate with more frosting or candies.

K.I.S.S. (Keep It Super Simple) Method: Use our pattern for the Chinese Lantern Teapot Lamp to add lid, spout and handle.

Homemade Fondant

One of the "miracle" materials for decorating cakes is a kind of sugar frosting that you can color and mold into shapes like modeling clay. Using fondant, you can create 3-D attachments like handles and spouts or surface decorations like polka dots or flowers. Think of it as an edible sculpture. Commercial, pre-rolled fondant and canisters of fondant are available from cake decorating suppliers for $10 - $16 per pound. But with a bit of practice, you can make your own.

What you need:

- 3 packages of unflavored, powdered gelatine (a total of 21.6 grams)
- Cold water
- 100 grams/3.3 ounces of fructose
- 1 Tablespoon glycerine
- 2 pounds of powdered sugar
- Food coloring or flavoring oils as desired

Directions:

Dissolve the gelatine in ¼ cup of cold water and allow it to sit for 5-10 minutes. Mix fructose and 1½ Tablespoons cold water in a saucepan and heat, stirring gently, until it boils. Allow it to simmer for about 1 minute and remove from the heat. Stir in gelatine and glycerine.

Put half the powdered sugar in a mixing bowl and create a well in the center. Pour in the liquid mixture and stir together. While stirring, add the remaining sugar a cupful at a time, saving ½ cup for kneading.

Sprinkle the ½ cup powdered sugar on a pastry board or covered countertop and knead the warm mixture until it forms a smooth ball. Knead in color and flavor as desired.

Cover with a dishtowel and let it cool before working or store it in an airtight container (not refrigerated) for up to 3 days. The fondant is easier to roll and shape after it has set a few hours or overnight.

If it becomes too hard to work easily, microwave for 3-5 seconds to soften.

Two Traditional Teatime Recipes

These two recipes are traditional accompaniments with warm scones when serving a British-style afternoon tea. But both are handy toppings to incorporate in other tea party recipes. Lemon Curd makes a decadent filling between layers of cake. And a spoonful of Mock Devonshire Cream can replace basic whipped cream as a topping for a bowl of fresh fruit.

Lemon Curd

Makes 2 cups. Serves 6-8.

Ingredients:

- ¾ cup fresh lemon juice
- 1 Tablespoon grated lemon zest
- ¾ cup sugar
- 3 eggs
- ½ cup butter, cut into chunks

Directions:

In a saucepan, combine lemon juice, lemon zest, sugar, eggs and butter. Cook over very low heat until thick, about 10 minutes, stirring frequently. Cool before serving. Lemon curd can be refrigerated in an airtight container for up to a week.

Mock Devonshire Cream

This is an imitation of the traditional topping that originated in Devon County, England. Makes 2 cups. Serves 6-8.

Ingredients:

- ½ cup cream cheese, softened
- 3 Tablespoons brown sugar
- ¼ teaspoon salt
- 1½ cups whipping cream
- ¼ teaspoon vanilla extract

Directions:

In a large bowl, combine cream cheese, sugar and salt. Mix well. Gradually add the whipping cream. This is most easily done with an electric mixer but it can be done by hand. Store covered in the refrigerator until ready to serve.

This is a traditional topping on warm scones. But there are many other uses, such as a dipping sauce for fresh strawberries.

Mandarin Orange Scones

The traditional quick bread we call scones wasn't originally the large wedge flavored with fruit and nuts that many of us have come to love and expect at Country and Victorian style tearooms. Scones were originally a rather plain biscuit cut in rounds, usually served with butter, jam, lemon curd or Devonshire cream. This recipe by Amy Lawrence, owner of An Afternoon To Remember, reflects the modern preferences for a light, tender pastry with a bit of flavoring. It is delicious with Lemon Curd and Mock Devonshire Cream.

Makes about 15 scones

Ingredients:

For Scones:

- 3 cups all-purpose flour
- 2 Tablespoons baking powder
- ¼ cup granulated sugar
- 1 stick of unsalted butter
- ¼ to ¾ cup buttermilk
- ½ cup mandarin oranges
- Grated zest of one orange

For Glaze:

- 1 cup powdered sugar
- 3 Tablespoons orange juice

Directions:

Preheat oven to 400 ° F.

Puree ¼ cup of the mandarin oranges in a food processor. Cut the remaining ¼ cup in half. Set aside.

Mix together flour and sugar. Use pastry cutter to cut in butter. Mixture should resemble coarse cornmeal. Add zest, pureed mandarins and mandarin segments. Add enough of the buttermilk to make the mixture come together. If mixture is too dry add more buttermilk until it barely holds together.

Turn out on a floured board. Pat out gently, by hand, to about 1" thick. Cut with a small biscuit cutter or into triangles. Bake for 15-20 minutes, or until nicely browned. Glaze when they are cool.

Glaze:

Mix together powdered sugar and orange juice. Dip scones in glaze. Let set until glaze is dry.

From Amy Lawrence, owner of Afternoon To Remember
Published in her cookbook, "Drop By For Tea".

Section 5

Resources for Tea Lovers

Tea Limerick

by Nani Matana

People all over sip tea
It draws us as one family.
Take time in your day
Let cares fall away
As you feel the Oneness with me

Items In This Section:

Popular Tea Quotes	106
Would You Like To Read More About Tea?	110
International Tea Festivals	112
Tearooms Serving Afternoon Tea	113
Interesting Online Tea Websites	119
One Last Cup of Tea	122

A Few Tea Quotes By Some Of Our Favorite Writers

We've selected some popular tea quotes by well known authors that you can use to decorate for your tea parties, to create party games or to enjoy during your private, contemplative teatime.

"Peter was not very well during the evening. His mother put him to bed, and made some chamomile tea: "One table-spoonful to be taken at bedtime."

— Beatrix Potter, *The Tale of Peter Rabbit*

"We had a kettle; we let it leak:
Our not repairing made it worse.
We haven't had any tea for a week...
The bottom is out of the Universe."

— Rudyard Kipling, *The Collected Poems of Rudyard Kipling*

"But when we consider how small after all, the cup of human enjoyment is, how soon overflowed with tears, how easily drained to the dregs in our quenchless thirst for infinity, we shall not blame ourselves for making so much of the tea-cup."

— Kakuzo Okakura, *The Book of Tea*

"When the girl returned, some hours later, she carried a tray, with a cup of fragrant tea steaming on it; and a plate piled up with very hot buttered toast, cut thick, very brown on both sides, with the butter running through the holes in great golden drops, like honey from the honeycomb. The smell of that buttered toast simply talked to Toad, and with no uncertain voice; talked of warm kitchens, of breakfasts on bright frosty mornings, of cozy parlour firesides on winter evenings, when one's ramble was over and slippered feet were propped on the fender, of the purring of contented cats, and the twitter of sleepy canaries."

— Kenneth Grahame, *The Wind In The Willows*

"A simple cup of tea is far from a simple matter."

— Mary Lou Heiss, The Story of Tea: A Cultural History and Drinking Guide

"Christopher Robin was home by this time, because it was the afternoon, and he was so glad to see that they stayed there until very nearly tea-time, and then they had a Very Nearly tea, which is one you forget about afterwards, and hurried on to Pooh Corner, so as to see Eeyore before it was too late to have a Proper Tea with Owl."
— A.A. Milne, *The House at Pooh Corner*

"So inscrutable is the arrangement of causes and consequences in this world, that a two-penny duty on tea, unjustly imposed in a sequestered part of it, changes the condition of all its inhabitants."
— Thomas Jefferson, *Autobiography of Thomas Jefferson*

"Tea tempers the spirits and harmonizes the mind, dispels lassitude and relieves fatigue, awakens thought and prevents drowsiness, lightens or refreshes the body and clears the perceptive faculties."
— Lu Yu, *Classic of Tea: Origins and Rituals*

"Tea to the English is really a picnic indoors."
— Alice Walker, *The Color Purple*

"The spirit of the tea beverage is one of peace, comfort and refinement."
— Arthur Gray, *Little Tea Book*

"When the tea is brought at five o'clock
And all the neat curtains are drawn with care,
The little black cat with bright green eyes
Is suddenly purring there."
— Harold Monro, *Collected Poems*

"There is something in the nature of tea that leads us into a world of quiet contemplation of life."
— Lin Yutang, *The Importance of Living*

"I take a few quick sips. "This is really good." And I mean it. I have never tasted tea like this. It is smooth, pungent, and instantly addicting.

"This is from Grand Auntie," my mother explains. "She told me 'If I buy the cheap tea, then I am saying that my whole life has not been worth something better.' A few years ago she bought it for herself. One hundred dollars a pound."

"You're kidding." I take another sip. It tastes even better.

— Amy Tan, *The Kitchen God's Wife*

"I can just imagine myself sitting down at the head of the table and pouring out the tea," said Anne, shutting her eyes ecstatically. "And asking Diana if she takes sugar! I know she doesn't but of course I'll ask her just as if I didn't know."

— L.M. Montgomery, *Anne of Green Gables*

"Though we eat little flesh and drink no wine,
Yet let's be merry; we'll have tea and toast;
Custards for supper, and an endless host
Of syllabubs and jellies and mince pies,
And other such ladylike luxuries."

— Percy Bysshe Shelley, *The Complete Poems*

"The Baroness found it amusing to go to tea; she dressed as if for dinner. The tea-table offered an anomalous and picturesque repast; and on leaving it they all sat and talked in the large piazza, or wandered about the garden in the starlight."

— Henry James, *The Europeans*

"Tea is one of the main stays of civilization in this country."

— George Orwell, *Smothered Under Journalism*

"It snowed last year too: I made a snowman and my brother knocked it down and I knocked my brother down and then we had tea."

— Dylan Thomas, *A Child's Christmas in Wales*

"A man who wishes to make his way in life could do no better than go through the world with a boiling tea-kettle in his hand."

— Sydney Smith, *A Memoir of the Reverend Sydney Smith*

"Presently, out from the wrappings came a teapot, which caused her to clasp her hands with delight, for it was made in the likeness of a plump little Chinaman ... Two pretty cups with covers, and a fine scarlet tray, completed the set, and made one long to have a "dish of tea," even in Chinese style, without cream or sugar."

— Louisa May Alcott, *Eight Cousins*

"This meal happened to be a make-believe tea, and they sat 'round the board guzzling in their greed; and really, what with their chatter and recriminations, the noise, as Wendy said, was positively deafening."

— J.M. Barrie, *Peter Pan*

"Rainy days should be spent at home with a cup of tea and a good book."

— Bill Watterson, *The Calvin and Hobbs Tenth Anniversary Book*

"Meanwhile, let us have a sip of tea. The afternoon glow is brightening the bamboos, the fountains are bubbling with delight, the soughing of the pines is herd in our kettle. Let us dream of evanescence and linger in the beautiful foolishness of things."

— Kakuzo Okakura, *The Book of Tea*

Would You Like To Read More About Tea?

This is a sampling of some of the diverse tea topics by dedicated tea writers.

Antol, Marie Nadine. *Healing Teas: How To Prepare and Use Teas to Maximize Your Health.* Avery Publishing Group, 1996.

Barnes, Emilie and Buchanan, Anne Christian. *The Twelve Teas of Friendship.* Harvest House, 2001.

Caldicott, Carolyn. *Vintage Tea Party.* Frances Lincoln, 2012.

Chuen, Master Lam Kam. *The Way of Tea: The Sublime Art Of Oriental Tea Drinking.* Gaia Books, 2002. Published as part of Barron's Educational Series.

Cousineau, Phil and Hoyt, Scott Chamberlin. *The Soul and Spirit of Tea.* Talking Leaves Press, 2013.

Donaldson, Babette. *Everything Healthy Tea.* Adams Media, 2014.

Fellman, Donna and Tizer, Lhasha. *Tea Here Now: Rituals, Remedies, and Meditations.* Inner Ocean Publishing, Inc. 2005.

Fisher, Aaron. *The Way of Tea: Reflections on a Life with Tea.* Tuttle Publishing, 2010.

Fong, Roy. *The Great Teas of China.* Tea Journey Books, 2009.

Gascoyne, Kevin. *Tea: History, Terroirs, Varieties.* Firefly Books, 2011.

Gold, Cynthia and Stern, Lise. *Culinary Tea.* Running Press, 2010.

Gustafson, Helen. *The Agony of The Leaves: The Ecstasy of My Life with Tea.* Henry Hold and Company, 1996.

Gustafson, Helen. *The Green Tea User's Manual.* Clarkson Potter, 2001.

Heiss, Mary Lou and Hess, Robert J. *The Story of Tea: A Cultural History and Drinking Guide.* Ten Speed Press, 2007.

Heiss, Mary Lou and Hess, Robert J. *The Tea Enthusiast's Handbook: A Guide to Enjoying the World's Best Teas.* Ten Speed Press, 2010.

Hendrickson, Kim. *Tastefully Small Finger Sandwiches: Easy Party Sandwiches for All Occasions.* Atlantic Publishing Group, 2008.

Hohenegger, Beatrice. *Liquid Jade: The Story of Tea from East to West.* St. Martin's Press, 2006.

Hoyt, Scott Chamberlin. *The Meaning of Tea: A Tea Inspired Journey.* Talking Leaves Press, 2009.

Johnson, Dorothea. *Tea & Etiquette: Taking Tea for Business and Pleasure.* Capital Books, 2000.

Kakuzo, Okakura. *The Book of Tea.* Tuttle Company, 1956.

Lawrence, Amy N. *Creating An Afternoon To Remember*. ATR Publishing, 2007.

Lawrence, Amy N. *Drop By For Tea*. ATR Publishing, 2008.

Lawrence, Amy N. *Twelve Teas To Remember*. ATR Publishing, 2013.

Peltier, Warren. *The Ancient Art of Tea: Wisdom from The Ancient Chinese Tea Masters*. Tuttle Publishing, 2011.

Martin, Laura C. *Tea, the Drink that Changed The World*. Tuttle Publishing, 2007.

Munichiello, Katrina Avila. *A Tea Reader: Living Life One Cup at a Time*. Tuttle Publishing, 2011.

Pettigrew, Jane. *The Social History of Tea*. Benjamin Press, 2013.

Pettigrew, Jane. *The Tea Companion (Connoisseur's Guides)*. Running Press, 2004.

Pettigrew, Jane and Richardson, Bruce. *The New Tea Lover's Companion*. Benjamin Press, 2008.

Pratt, James Norwood. *The Ultimate Tea Lover's Treasury: The Classic True Story of Tea*. Tea Society 2009.

Richardson, Lisa Boalt. *Tea with a Twist: Entertaining and Cooking with Tea*. Harvest House, 2010.

Richardson, Lisa Boalt. *The World in Your Teacup: Celebrating Tea Traditions, Near and Far*. Harvest House, 2010.

Rose, Sarah. *For All the Tea in China: How England Stole the World's Favorite Drink and Changed History*. Penguin Books, 2010.

Stuckey, Maggie. *Country Tea Parties*. Storey Publishing, 1996.

Zak, Victoria. *20,000 Secrets of Tea: The Most Effective Ways to Benefit from Nature's Healing Herbs*. A Dell Book, 1000.

Fun With Tea At
Tea Festivals Around The World

Boseong Green Tea Festival, Besong, South Korea — www.dahyang.boseong.go.kr

Coffee & Tea Fest Philly, Philadelphia, PA, USA — www.CoffeeAndTeaFestival.com/philly

Dublin Coffee & Tea Festival, Dublin, Ireland — www.DublinCoffeeFestival.com

First Flush Festival, Charleston, SC, USA — www.CharlestonTeaPlantation.com

Hong Kong International Tea Festival, Hong Kong, China — www.HKTDC.com/fair

Las Vegas Tea Festival, Las Vegas, NV, USA (Annual event but no current website.)

Los Angeles International Tea Festival - LA, CA, USA — www.TeaFestivalLA.com

New York Coffee and Tea Festival, New York, NY, USA — www.Coffee And Tea Festival.com

Northwest Tea Festival - Seattle, WA, USA — www.NWTeaFestival.com

Ottawa Tea Festival - Ottawa, Canada — www.OttawaTeaFestival.com

Portland Tea Festival, Portland, OR, USA — www.TeaFestPDX.com

Tea Festival of Assam, Jorhat, Assam, India (Annual event but there is no unique website.)

Tea Lovers Festival - Los Angeles, CA, USA — www.TeaLoversFestival.com

Rocky Mountain Tea Festival, Boulder, CO, USA — www.RockyMtnTeaFestival.com

San Francisco International Tea Festival - SF, CA, USA — www.SFInternationalTeaFestival.com

Teapot Days, Tea, SD, USA — www.teasd.com

Toronto Tea Festival - Toronto, Canada — www.TeaFestivalToronto.com

Vancouver Tea Festival - Vancouver, Canada — www.VancouverTeaFestival.ca

World O-Cha - Shizuoka, Japan — www.Ocha-Festival.jp/english

Xiamen Tea Festival - Xiamen, Fujian, China — www.TeaFair.com.cn/en

Some U.S. Tearooms Serving Afternoon Tea

Looking for an afternoon tearoom near you? Here we offer more than 200 suggestions but know that there are many more wonderful teas to discover. We'll be looking for updates to our list. Check our Fun With Tea website for more tearooms who welcome all ages.

Alabama

Charming Teacup, Point Clear
Emma's Tea Room, Huntsville
Heart's Desire Tearoom, Wilsonville
Smith-Byrd House, Prattville
Spiced Pear Tearoom, Homewood

Alaska

Highland Glen, Anchorage
Sipping Streams Tea Company, Fairbanks

Arizona

Arizona Biltmore, Phoenix, AZ
English Rose, Carefree
Kimberly Ann's Tea Room, Glendale
Ritz-Carlton, Phoenix
Seven Cups, Tucson
Souvia Tea, Phoenix
Tea Court at the Phoenician, Scottsdale
The Urban Tea Loft, Chandler

Arkansas

Chantilly's Tea Room, Harrison
Crumpet Tea Room, Rogers
Crumpet Tea Room Express, Bentonville
Simply Scrumptious Tea Room, Eureka Springs
The Empress, Little Rock
The English Tea Room, Siloam Springs
The Paper Rose Tea Room, Eureka Springs
The Tea Room at Vinson Square, Rogers
Wicks & Wax, Little Rock

California

August Tea Room, Diablo
Belladonna Tea Room, Lancaster
Bloomsbury Tea Room, Capitola
Camellia Tea Room, Benecia
Columbia Kate's, Columbia
Crown and Crumpet, San Francisco
Elise's Tea Room, Long Beach
Enchanted Rose, San Dimas
Golden Tea Garden, Hayward
High Tea Cottage, Woodland Hills
Lady Effie's Tea Parlor, Los Angeles
Linde Lane Tearoom, Dixon
Lisa's Tea Treasures, Campbell
Lovejoy's Tea Room, San Francisco
Paris In A Cup, Orange
Past Tyme Tea Parlour, Whittier
Possibili-Teas, Pioneer
Rose Tea Cottage, Pasadena
Scarlet Tea Room, Pasadena
Secret Garden Tea House, San Francisco
Silver Teapot, Manteca
Tranquility Tea Room, Thousand Oaks
Tea and Sympathy, Costa Mesa
Tea and Teacups, Yorba Linda
Tea Cozy, Cambria
Tea Time At The Mansion, Auburn
Tea Upon Chatsworth, San Diego
Tea With Friends, Livermore
The AubreyRose Tea Room, La Mesa
The English Rose Tea Room, Pleasanton
The French Bakery, Lafayette
Two A Tea, Glendora
Vintage Tea Leaf, Long Beach

Colorado

The Dusty Rose Tea Room, Georgetown
Boulder Dusahanbe Teahouse, Boulder
Mrs. B's Tea Parlor, Litton
Wisdom Tea House, Monument
The Castle at Glen Eyrie, Colorado Springs
Nan's Elizabeth Tea Room, Elizabeth

Connecticut

Celebrations, Pomfret Center
Mrs. Bridges Pantry, South Woodstock
Savvy Tea Gourmet, Madison
The Blossom, Greenwich
Tea Roses Tea Room, Cromwell
The Drawing Room, Cos Cob

Delaware

British Bell, Newark
Magpie Tea Garden, Wilmington
Middleburgh Colonial Tea Room, Wilmington
Tea For Two, Dover
The Victorian Lady, Milford

District of Columbia

British Pantry
Empress Lounge at the Mandarin Hotel
Four Seasons Hotel
Henley Park Hotel
Hillwood Cafe at Hillwood Museum
Lady Camellia
Mayflower Hotel
Peacock Alley Tea
Ritz-Carlton
Tea at the National Cathedral
Tea on the Tiber
Teaism
The Willard Hotel
The Mansion in Dupont Circle

Florida

Moffat's Cup of Tea, Dunedin
Southern Belles TeaRoom, Plant City
Tea Rose Cottage Tea, Tampa
The Empress Tea Room, Tampa
The Royal Tearoom, Tampa
Victorian Grace, Brandon
Wisteria Tea Room, Fort Myers

Georgia

Madison Tea Room, Madison
Sarah Belle Tea Room, Conyers
The Potted Geranium, Greensboro
Tea Leaves and Thyme, Woodstock
The Roswell Teahouse, Roswell
The Baron York, Clarkesville

Hawaii

A Cup of Tea, Kilua
Aloha Harmony Tea House, Honolulu
Halekulani Tea Room, Honolulu
Lisa Rose Doll House & Tea Room, Honolulu
Tea at 1024, Honolulu

Idaho

Miss Tami's Tearoom, Meridian
Stillwater Mansion, Idaho Falls

Illinois

Calla Lily Victorian Tea Room, Aurora
Country Thyme Tea Room, Paxton
Crumpet's Tea Room, Genoa
LaTeaDa Tea Room, Clinton
Pickwick Society Tearoom, Frankfort
Pinecone Cottage Tea House, Downers Grove

Indiana

Tina's Traditional Old English Kitchen, Danville
Twigs & Sprigs Tearoom, Commiskey

Iowa

Miss Spencer's Special Teas, New Virginia
Rose Cottage Tea Room, Clear Lake
Shay's Tea Room, Newton

Kansas

Castle Tea Room, Lawrence
Cup 'N Saucer, Wichita
Madam Hatter's Tea Room, Eudora
Mitzy London's Tea Room, Leawood
Cottage Rose Tea, Olathe
Strawberry Hill's Tea Room, Kansas City
Tea Market, Kansas City

Kentucky

2 Sisters Tea Room, Vine Grove
Candleberry Tea Room, Frankfort
Magnolia Tea Room, Hazel
Mrs. Teapots Tea Room, Belleview
Sisters Tea Parlor, Buckner
Yesterday's Tea Room, Florence

Louisiana

Bottom of The Cup, New Orleans
English Tea Room, Covington
Glenwood Village Tea Room, Shreveport
La Petite Tea Room, Metairie
Rose Garden Tea Room, San Marino,
The English Tea Room, Covington
The Glenwood Village Tearoom, Shreveport
The Lewis House Tea Room, Ruston
Vianne's Tea House, Mandeville

Maine

Garden Gate Tea Room, Acton
Jacqueline's Tea Room, Freeport
The Clipper Merchant, Limerick
Victorian Lace Tearoom, Burnham

Maryland

Reynolds Tea Room, Annapolis
Serenity Tea Room, Frederick
Sweet Simplici-Tea, Sykesville
Tea By Julia Faye, Baltimore
Tea By Two, Bel Air
Tea on The Tiber, Ellicott City
The Royal Tea Room, La Plata

Massachusetts

Fancy That, Walpole
Florabunda Tea Room, Rutland
Heath's Tea Room, Rockport
Nana B's Tea Room, Southbridge
The Dunbar Tea House, Sandwich
The Tea Leaf, Waltham
Tickle's Tea Room, Swansea
Triangle Tea Life, Provincetown
Wenham Tea House, Wenham
Windsor Tea Shop, Cohasset

Michigan

Celadon Gardens, Davisburg
Crazy Wisdom Tea Room, Ann Arbor
Sue & Esther's American Tea Room, Frankenmuth
Sweet Afton Tea Room, Plymouth
The Townsend Hotel, Birmingham
Tyme Well Spent Tea Room, Hartland

Minnesota

The Mad Hatter Tea Room, Anoka
Lady Elegant's Tea Room, St. Paul
The Avalon Tearoom, White Bear Lake

Mississippi

Fairview Inn, Jackson
Simply TeaVine, Hattiesburg
Martha's Tea Room, Ocean Springs
Miss Martha's Tea Room, Scottdale

Missouri

Henry's Antiques & Tearoom, Lee's Summit
Keepsakes Tea room, Belton
Memories on Main Street Tea Room

Montana

Chris' Tea Cottage, Bigfork
Scentsibili-Tea, Stevensville
Rebecca's Tea Room, Kalispell

Nebraska

Aunt Emma's Tea and Gifts, Sutton
Ruby & Cordelia's Fine Tea, Lincoln

Nevada

High Tea Society of N. Nevada, Carson City

New Hampshire

Cozy Tea Cart, Brookline
Pickety Place, Mason

New Jersey

600 Main Victorian Tearoom, Toms River
Amelia's Teas & Holly, Mullica Hill
Anna Beall's Tea Room
Chauncey Hotel, Princeton
Cozy Cupboard Tea Room, Convent Station
Harmony Tea Room, Westwood
High SocieTea House, Wayne
Mulberry Tea House, Medford
New Leaf Tea Room, Riverton
One Steep At A Thyme, Jamesburg
Tea & Tranqulitiy, Tuckerton
Tea 4 U, Oakhurst
Tea Hive, Newton
Teaberry's Tea Room, Flemington

New Jersey, continued

The Butterfly Tea Room, Cape May
The Flanders Hotel, Ocean City
The Lillagaard Tea Room, Ocean Grove
The Lizzie Rose, Tuckerton
The Picket Fence Tearoom, Haddonfield
Through The Looking Glass, Historic Smithville
Tranquil Garden Tea Room, Ocean Grove
Twining's Tea Room, Cape May

New Mexico

A Gathering of Angels, Cedar Crest
Figments Tea Shoppe, Albuquerque
St. James Tea Room, Albuquerque
Victorian Tea Room, Las Cruces

New York

A Spot of Tea, Rhinebeck
Alice's Tea Cup, New York
Caramoor Rosen House, Katonah
Casablanca Tearoom, New York
Charlotte's Tea Room, Warwick
Cup & Saucer Tea Room, Beacon
Girleez Etc., Manlius
Grammie's Pantry Tea Room, Skaneateles
Josephine's Victorian Tea Room, Lancaster
La-Tea-Da!, Rochester
Lady Mendl's, New York
Rose Garden Tea Room, Endicott
St. Regis Hotel, New York
Tanzy's Tea Room, Hudson
Tea and Sympathy, New York
The Secret Garden, Port Jefferson

North Carolina

A Garden Room Tea Room, Burlington
Afternoon Tea at O. Henry Hotel, Greensboro
Alice's Place, Winston-Salem
Calibash Garden Tea Room, Salisbury
Chelsea's, Asheville
Duncan Hill Inn Tea Room, Kannapolis
Green Gables Tea Room, Beaufort
Lady Bedford's Tea Parlour, Pinehurst
The Olde English Tea Room, Wake Forest
Savannah's On Main, Hendersonville
The Pegg House Tea Room, Kernersville
The Secret Tea Room, Greensboro
Wilmington Tea Room, Wilmington
Timeless Tea, Roanoke Rapids

North Dakota

221 Melsted Place, Mountain
Tea and Tranquility, Bismark
Sanctuary Guest House Tea Room, Walhalla

Ohio

BarleyTwist Tea Garden, Columbiana
Biddies, Dublin
Churchill's Fine Teas, Cincinnati
Clara J's at 219, Maumee
D's Victorian Teas, Bellbrook
Dragonfly Tea Room, Canal Fulton
Edith Mae's Tea Room, Xenia
Elaine's Tea Shoppe, Toledo
Emerald Necklace Inn Tea Room, Cleveland
Hannaford House Tea Room, Wilmington
Honeybee Tea Parties, Kent
Miss Molly's Tea Room, Medina
Pinkie's Up Tea House, Troy
Remember When, Kirtland
Southern Gardens Tea Room, Akron
Strawberries and Daydreams, Miamisburg
Sweet Shalom Tearoom, Sylvania
Tea & Thyme, Akron
Tea By The Sea, Lakeside
The Tea Caddy of Jackson, Jackson
The Tea Parlor, Liberty Township
Twin Creek Tea Room, West Alexandria

Oklahoma

Belvedere Mansion Tea Room, Claremore
Country Dove Tea Room, Elk City
Dane's Decor & Tea Room, Oklahoma City
Dragonmoon Tea Company, Tulsa
Grangeville Rose Tea Room, Shawnee
Inspirations, Edmond
Memory Lane Tea room, Owasso
Red Raspberry Tea Room, Nicoma Park
The Rose Garden, Oklahoma City
The Victorian Tea Room, Guthrie

Oregon

Berry Sweet Tea Parties, Beaverton
Carmelle's Tea Room, Salem
Cheryl's Cup of Tea, Oregon City
Julia's Tea Parlor, Salem
LaTeaDa, Tillamook
Lavender Bleu Tea Room, West Linn
Lisa's Tea Room, Philomath

Oregon, *continued*

Lovejoy's, Florence
Mademoiselle Noelle's Tea House, Portland
Serendipitea, Lincoln City
Sweet Tea Parties, Oregon City
Tea's Me, Hillsboro
The Doll House Tea Room, Milwaukie
The Hazel Room, Portland
Wakai Tea Room, Portland

Pennsylvania

Abigail's Tea Room, Reading
AntiquiTea, Pittsburgh
Camellia's Sin Tea Parlor, Carlisle
Gilbertsville Tea Room, Gilbertsville
Lady Bug Tea Room, East Berlin
Olivia's Tea Room, Camp Hill
Pamela's Victorian Tea, Bellwood
Simpson House Tea Room, Chester Springs
Sugar's Tea Room, Forty Fort
Sweet Remembrances, Mechanicsburg
The Front Porch Tea Room, Hallam
The GGS Hat & Gloves Tea Room, Mohnton
The Painted Teacup, Upper Darby
The Talking Teacup, Chalfont
The Tea Trolley, Delta
The Victorian Parlor, Spring Grove

Rhode Island

Pastiche, Providence
Spring Seasons Tea Room, Newport
Tea For You, Hope Valley

South Carolina

Anna's Arbor, Chester
English Country Tea Rooms, Greenville
Hopsewee Plantation Tea Room, Georgetown
Laura's Tea Room, Ridgeway
McCray Tea House, McCormick
Miss Fannie's Yesteryear Tea Room, Union
Ragamuffins Tea Room, Greenville
River Oak Cottage, Hopsewee Plantation
Tealoa, Greenville
The Cypress Inn TeaRoom, Conway
This Whole House, Summerville
Time Well Spent, Summerville

South Dakota

Custer Mansion, Custer
DeHoek Tea, Sioux Falls

Tennessee

Beyond The Garden Gate, Ooltewah
Cozy English Tea Room, Hixson
Dora Victoria's Tea Room, New Market
English Garden Tea Room, Gallatin
English Rose Tea Room, Chattanooga
Homestead Manor, Thompsons Station
Lady Marpelet's Tea Room, Cookeville
Miss Melanie's Tea Room, Johnson City
Mrs. Potts' Playhouse, Dickson
Rosebriar Dining, Eads
Scarlett's Garden Tea Room, Mt. Juliet
Tea On The Mountain, Tracy City
Wisteria Tea Room, Arlington

Texas

Alvin Tea Room, Alvin
Annie's Tea Room, Alvin
Bawdsey Manor, San Antonio
Beatitudes Tea Room, Grapevine
Four Friends, Pearland
Holly Berry Tea Room
Into My Garden Tea Room, Plano
Kay's Tea Parlour
Mad Hatter's Tea Room
Merry Heart Tearoom, Granbury
Milk Pail Bistro
Nee Nee's Tea Room
McHugh Tea Room, Houston
River House Tea Room
Serenitea Tea Room, Sugarland
Silver Sycamore, Pasadena
St. Regis Hotel, Houston
Texas Specialtea Shoppe, Waller
The Adolphus, Dallas
The Charleston Tea Room
The Chestnut Tree, Denton
The Teapot Depot, Highlands
The Whistle Stop Tea Room, Tomball
Your Cup of Tea, Houston

Utah

Desert Dove Tea Room, St. George
Protea Cottage, West Jordan
Tea Grotto, Salt Lake City
Teas 'n You, Farmington
The Beehive Tearoom, Salt Lake City

Vermont

Brandon Music Cafe, Brandon
Governor's House, Hyde Park
Rose Arbor, Chester

Virginia

1817 Norvelle-Otey House, Lynchburg
Anne Hathaway's Cottage, Staunton
Aylesbury Tea Room, Leesburg
Briar Patch Tea Room, Poquoson
British Pantry, Aldie
Camella's Remember When, Abingdon
Crest Hill Tea Room, The Plains
Feathernesters Tea Room, Richmond
Gourmet Briar Patch, Prince George
Little Apple Pastry Shop, Aldie
Madison Tea Room, Warrenton
Miss Minerva's Tea Room, Culpeper
Mrs. Hardesty's Tea Room, Harrisonburg
Peacock Manor, Lynchburg
Petticoats & Petit Fours, Roanoke
Pinkadilly Tea, Fredericksburg
Ritz-Carlton, Pentagon City
Ritz-Carlton, McLean
Robins Tea House, (Lewis Ginter) Richmond
Rosemont Manor, Berryville
Simply Tea, Amelia
Taste Tea Salon, Williamsburg
Tea With Mrs. B, Falls Church
The Blue Willow Tea Room, Petersburg
The Coach & Horses Tea Room, Winchester
The English Rose Tea Room, Virginia Beach
The Pink Bicycle Tea Room, Occoquan
The Ploughcroft Tearoom, Lynchburg
Things I Love, Manassas
Toodles Tea Room, Montpelier
Twisted Branch, Charlottesville
Victorian Station, Hampton
White Oak Tea Tavern, Troutville

Washington

Afternoon To Remember, Bothell
Attic Secrets, Marysville
Brambleberry Cottage, Spokane
Cederberg Tea House, Seattle
Elizabeth & Alexander's, Bothell
Hawthorn Tea Room, Tacoma
Makezie's Tea Room, Marysville
Perennial Tea Room, Seattle
Queen Mary Tea Room, Seattle
Ruby Sue's Tea and Treasures, La Conner
Silver Spoon Tea House, Spokane
Steeped In Comfort, Lakewood
Tea-4-2, Puyallup
The Crumpet Shop, Seattle
The Hawthorn Tea Room, Tacoma
Tea Room at Port Gamble, Port Gamble
The Secret Garden Tea Room, Sumner
Victorian Rose Tea Room, Port Orchard
Village Tea Company, Bothell

West Virginia

Crumpets and Tea, Huntington
Eckhart House Tea Room. Wheeling
Ferguson's Tea Room, Hurricane
Once Upon A Tea Room, Mannington
Serenity Tearoom, Frederick
Shaharazade's Tea Room, Shepherdstown
Stella's Tea Room, Lewisburg
The Tea Cupboard, Cumberland
The Tea Shoppe at Seneca Center, Morgantown

Wisconsin

Johanna May's Fine Teas, Weston
Taking Time For Tea, Boyceville
The Pfister, Milwaukee
Waukesha's Spring House Tea Room

Wyoming

Willow Fence Tea Room, Cody
Nagle Warren Mansion, Cheyenne

Some Interesting Tea Sites On The Internet

T-Ching   www.TChing.com

An association of more than ninety respected tea writers who have contributed more than three thousand articles to this extensive site. Along with almost daily new posts is an archive that includes tea history and education with something for tea lovers of all kinds.

World Tea News   www.WorldTeaNews.com

The latest tea and most interesting news from around the world, organized in one central location. Weekly newsletters designed for the tea trade, are a fascinating look at the global markeplace.

Association of Tea Bloggers   www.TeaBloggers.com

This worldwide association features more than seventy tea bloggers, in many different languages, with a little something for everyone.

Afternoon Tea Across America   https://Groups.Yahoo.com/neo

Search for this lovely group when you reach the Yahoo Groups home page. You'll find recipes and fantastic themes for tea parties with photographs from member events.

TeaMap   www.TeaMap.com

TeaMap is a helpful resource for traveling tea lovers who want to find a good cup of tea at their favorite destinations, even if that may be just around the corner. Directory listings are provided by the retailers and then organized by city, state and country.

United States Tea Association   www.TeaUSA.com

The U.S. Tea Association makes tea interesting and fun, providing lovely photographs and interesting articles about tea and the latest health research.

Tea Association of Canada   www.Tea.ca

The Tea Association of Canada is organized to support the tea industry in their country but also provides a great deal of education about tea, as well as their professional Tea Sommelier course.

United Kingdom Tea Council   www.Tea.co.uk

Filled with tips for brewing and the latest facts on health, this site can keep you well entertained with a great deal of interesting content, with a European focus.

Indian Tea Association   www.IndiaTea.org

This is an extensive site about the teas of India, the growers, growing conditions, manufacture, auctions, and other more general aspects, including product health and safety. You can feel as if you get to know the people who craft these lovely teas by spending a little time browsing here.

The Sri Lanka Tea Board   www.PureCeylonTea.com

Search for everything you want to know about tea from Sri Lanka and the people who grow, manufacture and sell it. The website provides the latest information on their fine tea.

Tea Board of Kenya   www.TeaBoard.or.ke

Learn more about the tea industry in this African country. Much of the information they provide is about their current research to develop new cultivars and the growth of the tea industry there.

International Tea Cuppers Club   www.TeaCuppers.com

ITCC is a worldwide tea community of people who share a passion not only for the finest teas but also for contributing to the refinement and evolution of the tea industry. Members participate in innovative Cupping Events, Member Hosted Events, the Community Board and the ITCC newsletter.

International Tea Sippers Society   www.TeaSippersSociety.com

ITSS was created to help tea lovers of all preference and to connect directly with tea businesses, and join a network of fellow tea lovers for tea focused travel, tea education and other special events.

TeaChef   www.TeaChef.com

Adagio Teas hosts some of the highest ranked and most useful sites. In addition to Tea Map so that tea lovers can sip their way around the world, they provide this E-Cookbook with tea as an ingredient in every recipe.

Tea Guy Speaks   www.TeaGuySpeaks.com

Journalist, William Lengeman, posts frequent articles on a variety of interesting tea topics, including book reviews, how-to articles, fun videos and interviews with tea professionals.

Tea Pages   www.TeaPages.net

Katrina Avila Munichiello, the author of *A Tea Reader: Living Life One Cup At A Time*, and Senior Editor of Tea Magazine, shares regular blogs about her experiences working in the industry and her life as a tea lover.

Some Interesting Tea Sites On The Internet, *continued*

The Tea Maestro   www.TheTeaMaestro.blogspot.com

MSN calls Bruce Richardson "A leading tea expert involved in tea's American renaissance for over 20 years." His blog shares his experiences as a tearoom owner, author, publisher and historian.

The Devotea   www.TheDevotea.Teatra.de

Blogger, Robert Godden, aptly describes is blog as, "Lord Devotea's Tea Sprouts, In which life's eternal questions are ignored in favour of a cup of tea."

Tea House Times   www.theteahousetimes.com

A bi-monthly publication available online or per issue through our print-on-demand service.

Tea In Texas   www.teaintexas.com

Join 10,000+ Texans for savory picks of the best regional free & local cultural events and deals each week. Includes fun stories and contests sent to your email, don't miss a tea affair! Also includes tips, coupons, and tea events.

Fun With Tea   www.Fun-With-Tea.com

We hope you will visit our website often for new additions and resources for adding to your tea activities and tea knowledge. Based on this book, you will find new comments and suggestions, photo galleries and recipes. Purchasing the book makes you a lifetime member.

Using the Website, www.Fun-With-Tea.com

- Go to the home page.
- Click on *"Enter Here"* under Member Login.
- Use the password - ***TSipFun4You*** - to open access to the member area.
- Subscribe to the newsletter for updates in our growing FWT community.

One Last Cup of Tea Coloring Page

Coloring page created by Hans-Jürgen Krahl

May you always have walls for the winds,
a roof for the rain, tea beside the fire,
laughter to cheer you, those you love near you,
and all your heart might desire.

— An Irish Blessing

Come along inside….
We'll see if tea and buns can make the world a better place

Kenneth Grahame, *The Wind in the Willows*

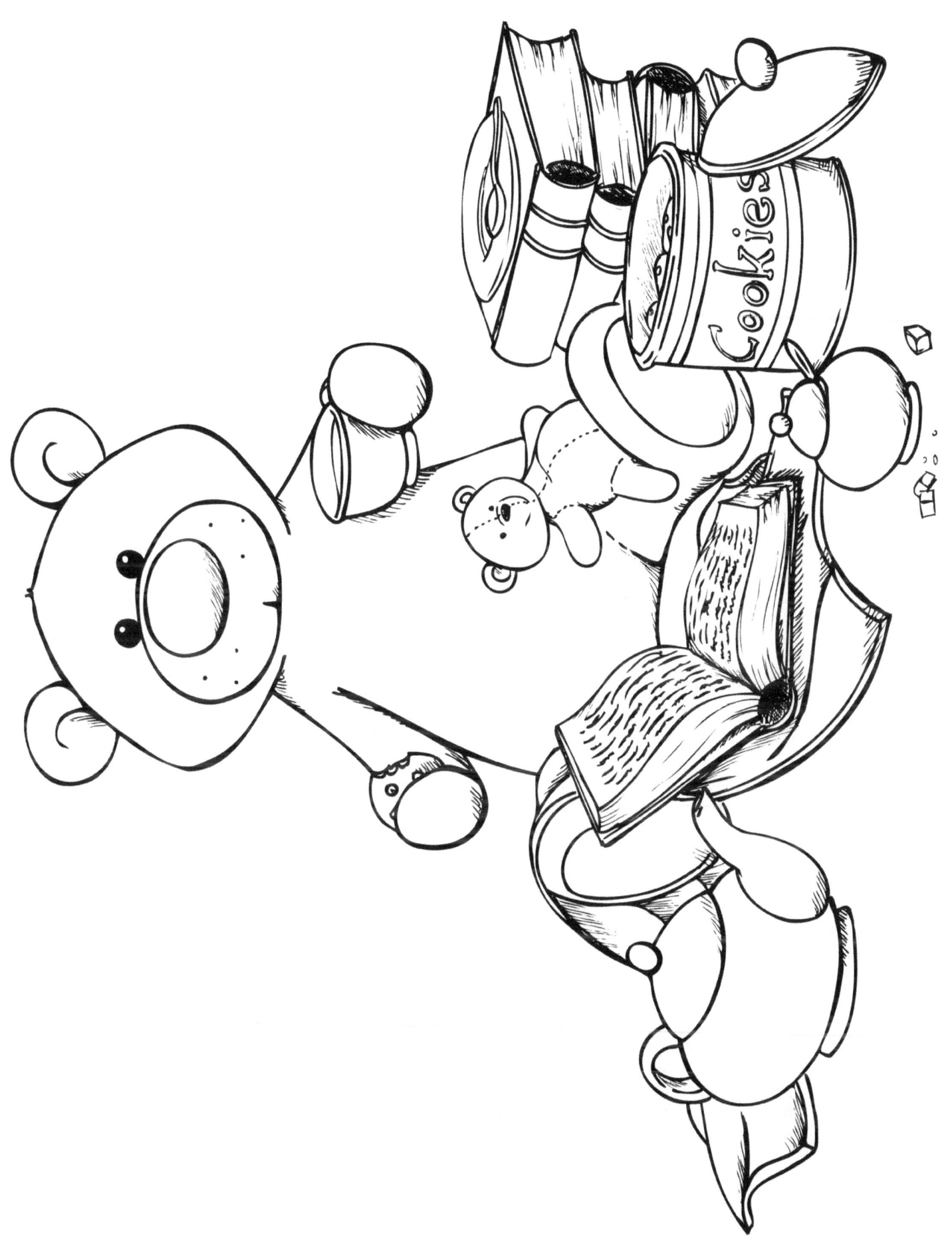

www.Fun-With-Tea.com